MAY–AUG

VOLUME 14 / PART 2

Edited by Grace Emmerson and John Parr

The Bible Reading Fellowship
OPENING THE BIBLE

Writers in this issue

The Pastoral Epistles **Leslie Houlden** is Emeritus Professor of Theology at King's College, London, and the author of numerous works on the New Testament and Christian belief.

Judges 1–8 **Stephen Dawes** is Chairman of the Cornwall District of the Methodist Church. Formerly he taught Old Testament and Hebrew at Trinity College, Legon, Ghana and at Queen's College, Birmingham.

John 1–6 **John Parr** is priest-in-charge of Harston with Hauxton and Newton, near Cambridge, and Continuing Ministerial Education Officer in the Ely Diocese.

Elijah and Elisha **Enid Mellor** is a specialist in Religious Education and has had many years' experience of teaching in schools and colleges of education, and in university departments of education, including King's College, London. Her published work includes *The Making of the Old Testament*, and a contribution to *Controversial Issues in the Curriculum*.

Peter and Jude **Anne Stevens** worked for the Civil Service and British Telecom before training for the Anglican ministry. Since her ordination she has worked as a curate in an inner-city parish in South London, and is now the Chaplain of Trinity College, Cambridge.

Job **Katharine Dell** is Assistant Lecturer in Old Testament Studies in the Faculty of Divinity at the University of Cambridge, and a Fellow of St Catharine's College. She is the author of two books on Job: *The Book of Job as Sceptical Literature* (1991), and *Shaking a Fist at God: Understanding Suffering through the Book of Job* (1995).

THE BRF *Magazine*

The BRF Prayer

O God our Father,
in the holy scriptures
you have given us your word
to be our teacher and guide:
help us and all the members of our Fellowship
to seek in our reading
the guidance of the Holy Spirit
that we may learn more of you
and of your will for us,
and so grow in likeness to your Son,
Jesus Christ our Lord.
Amen.

Editors' Letter

The selection of material in this issue shows some of the contrasts found in the Bible, as well as the connecting threads.

The Pastoral Epistles (1 and 2 Timothy and Titus) and Judges 1–8 come from widely different worlds. But they have a common theme. Leslie Houlden's notes on the Pastorals provide a glimpse of the church as it begins to settle down into the Roman world. Stephen Dawes' notes on the early chapters of Judges show how the tribes of Israel began to settle down in the promised land, and handle sensitively the problems raised by these ancient stories for today's Christians.

The gospel of John and the stories of Elijah and Elisha both come out of situations marked by tension and conflict: in the gospel, between the church and the synagogue, in 1 and 2 Kings between prophets and politicians. The notes on John 1–6 offer a fresh reading of the gospel based on some recent studies. Enid Mellor illuminates the faith and courage found in these gripping Old Testament stories.

The book of Job and the letters of Peter and Jude are about the struggle for faith, again in very different circumstances. Katharine Dell shares her reflections on a powerful work which courageously explores the problem of suffering in the world, and asks whether God intervenes in human life. Anne Stevens helps us to appreciate the plight of Christians whose faith brought them into serious conflict with the world around them, a world which they believed was coming to an end.

Contrasts and connections: worlds that are different from each other's and our own. The search and struggle for faith in today's world can be greatly enriched by eavesdropping on the conversations and correspondences found in the Bible. We hope that this will be your experience as you use this edition of *Guidelines*. Thanks to those who have written to us over the past few months. As ever, we value this contact with our readers. Your responses and suggestions not only encourage and help us in our work, but also deepen our sense of fellowship with you.

With all good wishes.

Grace Emmerson, John Parr
Guidelines Editors

Richard Fisher writes...

You will have read in the last issue of *The BRF Magazine* about the tragic and sudden death of Shelagh Brown in June 1997. Shelagh's funeral was held on Friday 18 July in Oxford. It was an occasion of real celebration of her life, and thanksgiving for all that she had achieved. Bishop Gavin Reid, Bishop of Maidstone and an old friend of Shelagh's, spoke at the funeral and a full transcript of his address can be found on page 8.

Thank you for the many hundreds of letters of sympathy and condolence that we have received from literally all over the world. We have been very conscious of being upheld by the prayers and support of so many of you. A Memorial Fund has been established in Shelagh's name which we believe will provide a lasting tribute to her. One of the main projects which the fund will support will be the Shelagh Brown Memorial Prize which will be awarded annually. At the time of writing (October 1997) details of the Prize are still being finalized, but we plan to publicize them in *The BRF Magazine* in due course. Donations to the Fund should be sent to BRF here in Oxford.

The Shelagh Brown Memorial Prize will be awarded annually

New Editor for *New Daylight*

We are delighted that David Winter has accepted our invitation to become Editor of *New Daylight*. David will be well known to many of you through his Bible reading notes, the bestselling 1995 BRF Lent book *What's in a Word?* or his regular radio broadcasting.

Staff News

As you will know from the last issue, the summer of 1997 was a time of great change for us in the BRF team. Shelagh died at the end of June, Chris Samways left us to move to Keynsham in mid-July, and in early August Andrew Starkie left to start ordination training at Ridley. And within six weeks, four new members of staff joined us! It is a great pleasure to introduce them now:

Naomi Starkey is the new commissioning editor for BRF's 'Bible Reading and Study' and 'Prayer and Spirituality' ranges. She will also be responsible for the *People's Bible Commentary* series. Lisa Field has taken over from Andrew as Assistant Editor, working on the entire BRF range of publications. Ann Knight has taken over from Chris Samways, looking after all our Group Secretaries. And Claire Laver has joined us to take up a new role on the team, looking after all our Individual Subscribers and working in BRF's accounts department. If you contact BRF by telephone, it is more than likely that you will speak to Ann or Claire. We are delighted, and deeply thankful to God, that at a time of such change and sadness we have been able to create such a strong new team to take the BRF work forward.

The Barnabas range for children continues to grow

New Publications

The *Barnabas* range (for children under the age of 11) continues to grow. The most recent additions are the first of the *Bible Days with Barnabas* series for 6–7s, and the *On the story mat* series for 5–6s. We have included an interview with 'Barny' on page 22. He will tell you all the latest news about the *Barnabas* imprint.

The next two volumes in the *People's Bible Commentary* have been published recently. *Luke* and *Nahum–Malachi* join the five volumes already available. An article about the series appears on page 16.

Let us know if you would like details of the full range of BRF publications, including all the new books, and we will send you the new adult, youth and children's catalogues.

CRE at Esher

The annual National Christian Resources Exhibition takes place from Tuesday 19 to Friday 22 May at Sandown Park, Esher. If you are able to visit the exhibition, do come and see us on the BRF stand. We would be delighted to see you.

And finally

We hope you will enjoy this issue of *The BRF Magazine* and the notes. Do continue to send us your letters and comments.

May you continue to know God's provision for you, his love and blessing throughout this year.

Address given by Bishop Gavin Reid at the funeral of Shelagh Brown

Friday 18 July 1997

Shelagh Brown was someone I thought I knew well… until I was asked if I would preach at her funeral and write her obituary… and then I realized that for all the hours we had spent together, and for all the ideas for books we had discussed, and for all the times we had sipped hock and put the world to rights, I knew remarkably little about her.

And yet there are some things that I can say about her with confidence, so here goes…

Shelagh loved people

One of her friends from Reigate has written: *Everything about Shelagh said 'welcome, you're so welcome into my home and my heart.'*

I remember the many visits I made to her little terraced cottage near Reigate. Whether I was with Mary, or whether I was alone, there was that tremendous sense of welcome. You felt that her only concern was to talk to you, affirm you, tease out the things that you were thinking about, put the world to rights, discuss theology, and latterly, dream up ideas for books; and during those times you felt that you were the only person that mattered to her! It was only when you joined one of her dinner parties that you saw she was exactly the same with all her friends. Perhaps it should not surprise us that a single person, who was so alive and excited about life, should love having other people around.

Shelagh loved nature

You will notice in her Bible reading note for 9 January (1997) the quotation from Gerard Manley Hopkins: 'The earth is filled with the grandeur of God'.

She loved that little house in Reigate. I think it must have been one of the most creatively untidy houses I have ever been in. But the french windows opened onto a large and lovely garden with a magnificent view of the North Downs. And the trees were her friends. She once told me that when she had to cut one down, she first asked for its forgiveness!

And there were other friends in that garden of hers.

Someone once wrote an article about her in the *Church Times*. The article mentioned the cat that was curled up in her lap. The following week's issue carried a letter from her which contained the following words:

'I do not possess a cat. I never have possessed a cat and I never shall. I don't like cats. Neither does the blackbird who squawks on my garden table every morning wanting his sultanas.'

Pam Rhodes once interviewed Shelagh for a *Songs of Praise* programme. They were sitting beside a river. Shelagh said, 'I love this river. When I was a child I used to play by it, and sometimes I just sat on the bank and looked at it.'

She loved sight and sound and taste and colour

Shelagh loved life

Somewhere around 1970 Shelagh went through a dramatic change of persona. When I first knew her she was very much the understated, evangelical single woman. She worked supportively for other people. She was the highly efficient secretary to Sir Norman Anderson. She dressed smartly but unremarkably. Then after the death of her parents an astonishing change came about. She bought her country house near Reigate. She bought a Triumph Spitfire sports car (or was it an MG), she started to wear suntan-effect make-up, she grew her hair longer, and out came those long, full Edwardian skirts, shirt tops, laced boots, beads galore, and deutero-Shelagh had arrived on the scene, and with what style!

I remember when I worked for Lutterworth Press. I asked the new Shelagh to join the editorial board. The first time she walked into the room where our rather stuffy little editorial board was shuffling its papers the conversation stopped, and every time she had something to say, they listened!

Somehow Shelagh had arrived as the person she had always wanted to be.

I remember calling to see her at Reigate. She was obviously in but there was no answer to my knocks at the door. Inside the house Shelagh was playing a record of 'Tie a yellow ribbon round the old oak tree'. She had turned the volume up to the limit, and she was singing and dancing round her living-room oblivious of the world outside.

And she could cook. Whether it be a full English breakfast—with kidneys, please note—or a delicious pan-fried steak and tossed salad—she knew what to do to make it special. She loved sight, and sound and taste and colour.

Shelagh loved the Bible

Her final years as commissioning editor for the Bible Reading Fellowship were the most fulfilling of her life. Not only was she working in the world of ideas and bringing books to birth, she was doing all that for the sake of the Bible, and she loved her Bible.

She rebelled over much of her evangelical background. Culturally, she found it too cramping for a single woman who wanted to love life, and to be something other than a member of the supporting cast, but she could never escape from the Bible and her love of it, and her conviction that it uniquely brought us into contact with the Word of God. She took very seriously the 80,000 readers of her Bible notes and she longed for them to be fed.

And I believe that when the full story is told, we may see that a great deal of the revival of the fortunes of the Bible Reading Fellowship can be traced to her efforts, and perhaps, if I ever have any claim to fame, it will be that I was the one who first persuaded Shelagh that she could write on her own account, and first commissioned something from her.

Shelagh loved getting her own way

On one occasion when Mary and I were about to tuck into one of her delicious suppers, the phone rang. Now I need to tell you that I have a submissive attitude towards phones that ring. Something inside me seems to cry out, 'Yes, master, I'm coming, master!' But not Shelagh. She paused for a moment and then said firmly, 'I don't think I want to speak with anyone else at this moment!' And the meal and the conversation continued, and eventually the phone gave up.

As an editor she had many gifts. She made her authors feel good about themselves. She had an infectious excitement about ideas and she had a nose for a good title. But her greatest gift was that she let very few authors escape! And it was no excuse to say that you had no time to write. She would simply produce her famous tape recorder and say, 'You say it and I'll write it for you.'

Her greatest gift was that she let very few authors escape!

My last memory of Shelagh was on the morning of 10 May this year. I had to leave the breakfast table at Bishop's House to do a school Confirmation. But she had that wretched recorder with her, and she was determined to get a contribution from me for a forthcoming book. So, while I gulped down my coffee, there she was asking questions and recording answers. I got the car out and went back to say goodbye. It was to be our last goodbye. I don't think Shelagh looked up. She was too busy recording Mary's contribution.

And even when she wasn't in as much control as she would like, she had the style to carry it off with dignity.

There was the occasion at the high altar of Southwark Cathedral, when a momentary lapse in concentration meant that she poured the wine into the ciborium and found herself staring down at seventy drowning wafers! Her response was typical. She picked up the vessel and solemnly walked into the wings and handed it to a startled verger!

But Shelagh also knew times when she was not in control and when she struggled with darkness and despair.

Amongst her personal papers is a revealing note written in October 1992, shortly before the General Synod was due to vote on the ordination of women. 'I am distressed and depressed,' she wrote, 'about the likely "no" vote in Synod. If, as seems likely, it is a "no" vote, I will cease to worship in the Church of England.' The entry goes on to record her plans for the day when the debate would take place: what she would do, where she would go and then came the words, '...so help, Holy Spirit... Jesus—please come alongside me to energize and enthuse me and to search out my rage and deal with it...' And then comes some pure Shelagh. The entry continues, 'Now I will assault the bedroom and the washing up as the Israelites launched their attack on the promised land!'

'We have had to let go of a very special person'

One of her Reigate friends wrote, 'Our hearts are heavy because we have to let go of a very special person.' Kriss Akabusi wrote, 'Although as a Christian I am aware that she has gone home, it does not make the loss of her in a foreign country any easier... Shelagh had so much that she wanted to do...' Her gardener said to a friend of hers, 'Miss Brown was a good lady, but He didn't look after her very well...'

Why, when she was so full of life and plans, did God allow her to fall to her death in her own home? And here I come to my text. Some words from St Paul's famous passage on love... 'For now we see in a mirror, dimly... but then we will see face to face.'

Of course we can all think of reasons why God was being kind in ending her life so suddenly. Shelagh hated the thought of growing old and was actually afraid of doctors and hospitals. In all the months since her return to Oxford, she has never registered with a doctor. She would have hated becoming frail and losing control. She would probably have had to be prized out of the job at BRF. But is that really the answer? If it is, why does God not despatch quickly all those others of his servants who seem to linger on for years—often with little apparent quality of life? And were the hundreds of thousands of Rwandan men, women and children who were massacred all being put out of some misery? No, we see in a mirror pretty dimly for a great deal of the time.

'Death... is a door to a life of glory that will last forever'

For all his confidence in God and in his gospel, it was St Paul who wrote that life, and God's ways, can be puzzling and perplexing. 'If our hope is only a hope for what happens in this life,' he wrote, 'we are, of all people, most to be pitied.'

But of course, the Christian holds firm to the conviction that life can never be understood with reference to the present. The present can only make sense in the light of the future. '*Now* we see in a mirror dimly, *then* we will see face to face. *Now* I know only in part, *then* I will know fully.'

Shelagh was totally convinced about this. Those who read her *New Daylight* note for 8 January this year (1997) would have read some vintage Shelagh.

It was simple. It was confident. It showed that for all her lifestyle changes and for all her new self assertedness, and for all her ability to converse with the John Robinsons and Tom Wrights of this world, Shelagh still believed the simple gospel that she had learnt all those years ago at All Souls Langham Place: *'Death isn't the end of everything for the Christian. It is a door to a life of glory that will last forever. We know that and believe it because the death of Christ on the cross wasn't the end of everything for him. He died—and his body was put in a tomb. But God raised him from the dead, and the tomb was left empty...'*

Well said, Shelagh, and all the people said—Amen!

Gavin Reid is Bishop of Maidstone, and co-author (with Shelagh Brown) of *Confirmed for Life*, published by BRF in 1996.

Hallowed be thy name

John Fenton

The Lord's Prayer must be one of the prayers that is said most frequently. At every moment, day and night, there must be someone, somewhere, who is saying it.

In Judaism at the time of Jesus, there was a prayer known as the *Shema*, which was said twice daily by adult Jewish males; and in an old Christian Church Manual (called *The Teaching of the Apostles*, possibly from the second century), where the Lord's Prayer is quoted, it is followed immediately by the instruction, 'Say this prayer three times every day.'

The prayer became part of the eucharistic liturgy in many of its forms, and it was frequently used as the basis for teaching people preparing to be baptized how to pray.

But the strange thing is that, for all its brevity, it has within it more matters on which writers have disagreed than any other passage of similar length.

Hallowed be thy name

One of these problems comes right at the beginning of the prayer with the words 'Hallowed be thy name.'

This has often been explained as a doxology, like the expression 'Blessed be he' that comes so frequently in Jewish writings after God has been mentioned. The traditional translation of the Lord's Prayer into English suggests this meaning; it gives the impression that this part of the prayer is different from the two lines that follow it: 'Thy kingdom come, Thy will be done.'

The order of words in Greek (in Matthew 6:9, 10) does not support this interpretation. Each of the three petitions is arranged in exactly the same order. Each begins with a verb (be hallowed, come, be done); then there is the definite article (the), with a noun (name, kingdom, will); and each petition ends with the word 'your'. In Greek there is even a rhyme between each of the first and the last words of these three lines.

Keeping the original order of words in Greek, we could translate it, absolutely literally, like this:

Be hallowed the name of you.
Come the kingdom of you.
Be done the will of you.

This has suggested to some of those who have studied the prayer recently that, just as the words are in the same order, so also the meaning of the petitions is continuous and repeated; that one thing is being asked for, in three similar ways. The prayer prays for the coming of the time when, firstly, God's name will be hallowed; secondly, his kingdom will come; and thirdly, his will will be done, on earth… It is like three knocks on the door, each meaning the same thing.

This way of understanding 'Hallowed be thy name', as a request for God to act, to rule the world in such a way that all other rulers are abolished, is supported by another fact about the words that are being used. They are almost a direct quotation from the Old Testament.

Jesus proclaimed… the time when God, not Satan, would rule

The proof that God cares

In the book of Ezekiel, God speaks through the prophet to the Israelites in exile and says:

It is not for the sake of you Israelites that I am acting, but for the sake of my holy name, which you have profaned among the peoples where you have gone. I shall hallow my great name, which you have profaned among those nations. When they see that I reveal my holiness through you, they will know that I am the Lord, says the Lord God. (Ezekiel 36:22, 23 REB)

The restoration of Israel to their own land will be the proof that God cares for his people; his 'reputation' will be restored, and people will see this, and honour his name:

The nations still left around you will know that it is I, the Lord, who have rebuilt the shattered towns and replanted the land laid waste; I, the Lord, have spoken and I shall do it. (36:36)

All of the first three gospels tell us that Jesus proclaimed the coming of the Kingdom of God, the time when God, not Satan, would rule. The casting out of evil spirits was a sign that this would happen; the strong man (Satan) was bound; his goods (the sick) were being rescued from his clutches.

The prayer that Jesus gave to his disciples was, therefore, for the fulfilment of what God was beginning to do. It takes us back, as we would expect, to the earliest days of the followers of Jesus, and shows us how their hopes were expressed at that time.

We are very close to a prayer that was said in the synagogues, which also mentions the sanctification of God's name, his kingdom and his will. It is called *The Kiddush*, and this is the translation of the beginning of it in *The Oxford Book of Prayer* (Ed. G Appleton, No. 842):

Let us magnify and let us sanctify the great name of God in the world which He created according to His will. May his kingdom come in your lifetime, and in your days, and in the lifetime of the family of Israel—quickly and speedily may it come. Amen.

May his kingdom come in your lifetime

Finish then thy new creation

To pray that God will sanctify his name is therefore to ask for the coming of the end of the way things are now, and to long for the future in which God's justice will be revealed. Anyone who believes in God will also experience the sense that all is not well with the world; all is not as it should be. To hope is to take this sense of the incompleteness of things as they are now, and to ask God to put them right. 'Finish then thy new creation.' It is partly a prayer for ourselves: 'Pure and spotless let us be.' But it is also (as Charles Wesley's hymn is not) a prayer for everything else in the world; it asks that God will do what John the Seer heard him say that he was doing: I am making all things new! (Revelation 21:5).

The People's Bible Commentary

Naomi Starkey

As a small girl, I was taught a chorus by my Sunday School teacher which consisted of just three lines: 'Read the Bible, pray every day, if you want to grow.' As a teenager, I ambitiously tried to read the Bible straight through, but I came unstuck somewhere in Leviticus. Bible reading notes of various kinds proved an easier way of combining study with prayer and reflection.

To leap ahead a few years (although not *that* many), I have found that, since joining the BRF team last August, I have gained a much deeper appreciation of how Scripture is indeed part of the foundation of Christian faith. And even before my arrival, I had noticed and been impressed by BRF's flagship series, the *People's Bible Commentary*.

The idea behind the series was conceived by the late and much-missed Shelagh Brown. As *New Daylight* editor, Bible teacher and author in her own right, Shelagh knew how ordinary Christians needed just the right tools to help them tackle Bible reading.

Through *New Daylight*, she made available an exceptional daily Bible reading resource for Christians of all ages. *Guidelines* was also available, tackling passages at a more testing level—but Shelagh was aware of a gap in BRF's output. Readers used to the theological breadth of BRF's daily notes could not find a commentary series with the same emphasis.

A number of popular series already existed, but they tended to cater for a fairly precise evangelical readership. Other commentaries were almost exclusively academic and heavyweight (in all senses of the word).

Shelagh had another passion: encouraging into Bible reading those Christians whose church background did not make it a priority. She wanted to pull together a team of authors for a series which would present a rich blend of tradition and interpretation, while always affirming the authority of the Bible.

She thought, too, of Bible study group leaders, and all the lay preachers and clergy needing user-friendly nuggets of insight, as weekly sermon deadlines loomed!

Thankfully, Shelagh lived to see her dream turn to reality as the first volumes of the *People's Bible Commentary* appeared to an enthusiastic response. Having become managing editor of the series, following Shelagh's sad and sudden death, my task is to ensure that the work is completed as she had planned. From November this year onwards, BRF will be publishing four commentaries a year, revising earlier titles as necessary.

So what are the unique characteristics of the series? Each volume takes a book or books of the Bible and divides it into daily readings and comment, together with a prayer or point for reflection. The authors come from a range of Christian backgrounds, including Anglicans, Methodists, Baptists and Roman Catholics, from the UK, Europe, USA and Australia. While most of them are involved in academic study at the highest level, they are hand-picked for their talent in communicating to a wide audience.

As the series develops, I am keen to see it used also as a study resource for new Christians. These days, many come to faith without the general Bible knowledge instilled by churchgoing childhoods. It is a privilege, but also a challenge, to introduce them to the Bible for the first time.

While many Christians, new and established, will find daily reading material such as *New Daylight* and *Guidelines* invaluable, others will want to explore further, focusing in detail on one Bible book at a time. They may well find a *People's Bible Commentary* volume a great help.

Another way in which the series can be helpful is in restoring the joy of Scripture all too easily forgotten by those in full-time Christian ministry. With their devotional focus, the *People's Bible Commentary* books can act as a useful reminder that, ultimately, the Bible is an expression of and pointer to the Word of God, to Jesus Christ himself.

Properly conducted, Bible study is a means of worship. As we study and learn to love the Bible more, so our love for God grows stronger. As our love for God grows, so does our love for others. Beyond all else, Shelagh's dream (and my aim in completing her work with the series) is to see that love grow, until every part of the world is touched and brought closer to God's healing presence.

Naomi Starkey is a commissioning editor for BRF and managing editor of the *People's Bible Commentary* series.

Volumes available now include *Genesis, Nahum–Malachi, Luke, Galatians, 1 Corinthians* and *Revelation*. All are available from your local Chritian bookshop or, in case of difficulty, direct from BRF using the order form on page 159.

Beginning where you are

Brother Ramon SSF

Sometimes people come to my hermitage with great sorrow in their hearts, looking for comfort; or with great joy, looking for enthusiastic fellowship; or with great yearning, looking for a deeper experience of God.

After much listening and some sharing, we go into my hut chapel and sit or kneel, bringing our sorrow, our joy, our profound yearning before the mystery of God. Then in silence, scripture and laying-on of hands, we experience the loving presence—and that presence means different things according to the need of the seeker.

You may come in need or emptiness, hardly knowing where to begin

For some, 'the presence' means the mysterious comfort-in-pain which wells up from the indwelling Spirit; for others it is the paradoxical tears-in-joy that come from the overflowing heart; for others it is a drawing-into-silence where their great yearning is rooted in simply being in God, where the soul begins a new chapter without words or images, but being taught by the Holy Spirit directly in the deeper reaches of prayer.

You may be able to identify with some of these people, or you may feel that you do not come with any deep feelings of sorrow, joy or yearning, but simply in need or emptiness, hardly knowing where to begin. Indeed, whenever you read of the tribulations and visions of 'great saints at prayer', or scan lists of retreats offering 128 techniques or 72 new approaches to posture, imaging or ecstatic meditation, you want to run away!

Part of me wants to say, '…don't worry about it—have no anxieties, just start where you are in the ordinary, simple joys and sorrows of daily life—put them into your own words, in your own style, in your own time, and God will lead you on.'

But another part of me wants to say, 'If you were wanting to learn to swim, ride a bike, drive a car or become computer literate you would have to give time, effort, concentration of body and mind and be willing to be taught—so in the art of prayer.' You see, it is all so simple, and yet it is a pilgrimage of a lifetime, 'from glory to glory advancing'.

The wonderful thing is that the deeper reaches of prayer are open to the simplest souls

Prayer and love

What I endeavour to do when people come to me is to listen to them, be aware of their body language, give myself simply to them in welcome and openness, so that I can see and hear and feel where they are. This means reading between the lines, hearing what they are not saying, and sometimes gently, sympathetically, lovingly, asking some questions, enabling them to be as open with me as I am with them.

Then, because I seek to live in an atmosphere of prayer and love, 'the word is given' and something will be said, or something will be imparted, so that the rubble will be cleared away and the water will bubble forth from the hidden spring, or the fire will begin to burn with a quiet flame.

Prayer is simple—it is we who are the complicated ones, and if only the seeker can remove the muck and sludge that blocks the channels, then prayer and love will flow—and be sure of this—there will be no real prayer unless love and compassion are part of the cleansing process.

An altar to God in our hearts

John Chrysostom said, 'No matter where we happen to be, by prayer we set up an altar to God in our hearts...' and that links beautifully with the whole hymn by Charles Wesley which begins:

O Thou who camest from above
The pure celestial fire to impart,
Kindle a flame of sacred love
On the mean altar of my heart.

The wonderful thing is that the deeper reaches of prayer are open to the simplest souls, and it is sometimes the case that theologians and clergy are so filled with verbalizing, information and cerebral dogmatizing that they are unable to discover the interior longing and silence which is the condition for the Holy Spirit's inner leading. I do not despise the application of the mind in the work of theology, for I have spent many years in such a pursuit, but we do not pray with our brains (nor with the undisciplined emotions) but with that intuitive approach of simplicity of mind and heart to which all the great mystics call attention.

> *It became a harmony of discipline and spontaneity, a tremendous sense of control and freedom*

A kiteful of lessons

Just two years ago a friend gave me a stunt kite, and I was excited as I opened the package, but was then perplexed and dismayed as I read the instructions. They spoke of launching, control, manoeuvres, flight manipulation, total depowering and landing. There was also an important and mysterious note on the angle and edge of the 'wind window'. I had little idea of what all this meant, but as I took over the flying, I discovered the meaning of the esoteric language in actual experience.

I really moved from basic to advanced control, from gradual smooth turns to sharper turns in my right and left hand and arm movements, in concert with the rising and falling wind. And I found that there was indeed an arc in which the kite functioned, and within that flying arc there was a centre and an edge of wind direction, which all made sense in the actual doing of it.

What was esoteric and inexplicable in the written directions become experientially clear and obvious as I allowed the wind to take me, the kite to direct me, and the lines to connect me to the whole activity. It became a harmony of discipline and spontaneity which gave me a tremendous sense of control and freedom, of joy and breathlessness, which was doubly rewarding—a whole kiteful of lessons!

At this point I should begin with some concrete and practical suggestions, leading you to begin to pray with nature, with scripture, with images, music, calligraphy, painting, walking or whatever you like to do. But the object of these paragraphs is simply to whet your appetite, so that you can go to a man or woman of prayer, take up a simple book of method, or start with something like The Jesus Prayer and simply move forward a step at a time.

When I saw some 'expert lads' kite-flying on Swansea beach, I longed to do the same. And by dint of enthusiasm, instructions and experience I can now fly a stunt kite with diving and swooping, figures of eight and reversals, with floating grace and exciting thrills and spills in the stunting.

So by watching, listening, reading and sharing The Jesus Prayer many years ago, I began where I was—and now it is the scriptural foundation of my life.

I have been led through darkness and light, through sorrow and joy, through pain and healing, into the depths of my own soul, into the sorrow and compassion of our world, and into the awesome mystery of God. And I've only just begun!

I've only just begun!

Brother Ramon is a Franciscan hermit who lives in solitude alongside a community in Worcestershire. He is a widely read and popular devotional writer.

For further reading:

The Jesus Prayer, Simon Barrington-Ward, BRF

The Heart of Prayer, Brother Ramon SSF, HarperCollins

Catch the bus!

There's no doubt who's the brightest bus in town—it's Barnabas. But what's life like when you suddenly find yourself in the fast lane? Our intrepid reporter stuck out a hand, hopped on board and found out what makes Barnabas tick.

How did you come to be travelling down this road, Barnabas?

Well, it's all in the name really. BRF were looking for someone to drive their children's books into the next century and I applied for the job. Barnabas means *son of encouragement*, you see, and that's what I love to do — encourage the kids to read the best book ever.

Which book's that, Barny?

The Bible, of course! My driver, Joe, gave me one for Christmas—it was a really cool present. He's always telling Bible stories to the children in our village. I like to sneak up to the church window and listen in.

Ah, so that's what you do on a Sunday!

You bet! And during the week I take the children to school—you can read all about my adventures in *Bible Days with Barnabas*. The stories are written by Taffy Davies—now there's a guy who knows how to catch your best side—though I'm no oil painting.

But I hear you're a bit of a live wire…

Ah, yes, but that's another story. Do you know, there's a computer in *Livewires* which takes the kids right into the Bible. I'm always amazed at how much I learn about the Bible through their adventures. People, places and stories galore… it's really cool. I jot down all our special outings on the diary pages. We went to a planet-

Barnabas, I do believe you're laughing!

I find I laugh quite a lot these days. Gone are the days when all I worry about is getting through my MOT. Nowadays, I feel that I'm in everyone's good books.

I can see you really enjoy being in print!

Being an imprint, you mean! My job is to look after all the kids up to 10, you know. I'll never 'tyre' of doing that—if you'll pardon the pun!

arium recently and then Taffy wrote a Bible Days adventure about it. It's called *Barnabas and the Stars*—all about how we are all part of God's family.

Well, you're a bit of a star, Barny and I get the impression that you really like Bible stories.

Oh, yes! They really make my plugs spark! Now there's some really brill stories by Brian Ogden coming out soon. *On the story mat* is the series and the first two books are *Sometimes the donkey is right* and *Best friends*. They're set in a reception class—the children are a bit younger than Miss Hollyoak's class in our village school, but I'm really fond of their teacher, Mrs Jolley. Wish all teachers were as nice as she is! Hoot! Hoot!

So what are your plans for the future, Barnabas?

Well, I'm making sure that everyone can come on board, you see. There are books for special times of the year like *The Advent Alphabet* and *Easter Treasure Hunt* and books for children to read by themselves like *Livewires* and *On the story mat*. Then there are books with lots of ideas for teaching programmes, like *The Ultimate Holiday Club Guide* and *Livewires LIVE*, which will be based on the first six of the *Livewires* volumes. Sometimes I get so excited by it all that my radiator boils over and Joe has to cool me down.

How can people find out where to catch up with you, Barnabas?

Well, I have my very own section of the BRF catalogue and all the latest books are in there. You can get one direct from BRF or from your local bookshop. Would you like me to drop you off outside? It's the next

stop and I'll be pulling up anyway to check they've got my latest titles in stock.

Barny was interviewed by Sue Doggett, BRF's children's commissioning editor. All *Barnabas* titles are available from your local Christian bookshop or, in case of difficulty, direct from BRF using the order form on page 159. For full details of the *Barnabas* range, write for the latest catalogue from BRF.

The Pastoral Epistles

The first and second letters to Timothy and the letter to Titus have long been thought of as belonging together, and known as 'the Pastoral Epistles'. The name is apt: they give solid guidance to Christian pastors about the organization and conduct of Christian congregations and their protection against false beliefs. They show Paul instructing Timothy and Titus—two of his lieutenants, apparently seen as supervisors of churches, like Paul himself—in these matters with a degree of detail and precision not found in the other Pauline letters. (Both men are known from the letters to the Corinthians, and Titus from Galatians.) It is no wonder that these documents have proved useful as guides and authorities for church leaders down the centuries, in matters like the structure of the ministry (1 Timothy 3) and the mode of ordination (1 Timothy 4:14).

The fact that these interests belong to the more settled life of the church rather than its initial phase (see 2 Timothy 1:5) has prompted the suggestion that these writings may not in fact be the work of Paul. Their emphasis on making sure of the church's frontiers and on projecting a peaceable image to outsiders (1 Timothy 2:2) seems more akin to writings of the second century than to those of Paul the missionary. So does the fact that the doctrinal statements about Christ seem formal and are detached from the practical teaching: in Paul's main letters all is integrated into a single vision. So too does the Greek vocabulary used here: it differs widely from that of Paul, suggesting that, even if this is his work, he was perhaps letting a secretary write things his own way.

Realization of these matters has led most scholarly opinion to the view that these writings are the work of a devotee of Paul, writing a generation or two after his life, that is, around the end of the first century, perhaps later. This should not shock us. In the ancient world, in the absence of copyright laws, the practice of writing in the name of another was far from unusual, and it was often done for the best of motives. Here we have a follower of Paul wearing his mantle and claiming his authority for what he felt to be important instruction. It was what, in his opinion, Paul would surely have said if he had still been alive. Some scholars would exempt 2 Timothy from this assessment, or feel that at least the intensely personal material in chapter 4 derives from genuine fragments of Paul's work. But it has to be said that the conventions of the time allowed for imagination to construct such material and examples abound from Christian writers of the subsequent period. Perhaps the significant general point for us about the Pastoral Epistles is that they then show a second- or third-generation Christian setting about the task of faithfully applying and adapting the tradition of his faith to new circumstances and new needs. That task has continued ever since and faces us still.

The notes are based on the Revised Standard Version of the Bible.

4–10 MAY 1 TIMOTHY 1:1—6:21

1 Taking a firm line *Read 1 Timothy 1*

This heading could stand as a summary of the Pastoral Epistles as a whole. After the conventional opening, the writer launches straight into a sequence of denunciations and warnings that plainly reflect matters close to his heart. It is interesting that he does not tell us much about the detailed views of those to whom he takes such strong exception, nor in fact do we hear much about the actual content of his own faith. Instead, the emphasis falls on the importance of conformity to orthodoxy in faith and morals, virtually for its own sake, and on the sheer wickedness of dissidence.

It is not an altogether pretty picture. Many modern readers are likely to feel that they have heard enough of this kind of narrowness, from numerous quarters. But uncongenial as the tone surely is, there is another side to the matter. Any community, if it is to stand for anything, must in due course draw boundaries round itself. The Christian community, as we see it in the undoubted letters of Paul, began with a vision that was boundless: it was for the entire human race, irrespective of race, gender and social status, and its ethic centred on selfless, outgoing love. What we have here is a reflection of a later stage, when the difficulties in sustaining or realizing that vision have come to the fore. Are these not dilemmas that face the church—and indeed individuals—in every age? This is an early instance of the problem expressed in the title of David Lodge's novel about Roman Catholics at the time of Vatican II with its liberal reforms: *How Far Can You Go?*

It is instructive to see how the writer uses Pauline 'scenery', but repaints it. In verse 8, we learn that 'the law is good' because it condemns evil and separates good people from the wicked. Paul was more subtle and more profound: all are sinners and are in need of redemption; and law is both good and destructive. And contrast verse 20 with 1 Corinthians 5:5, where hope of salvation remains open to an offender. Paul's vision is both positive and open. The writer of this letter shows us what happens when good men, in charge of affairs, bring smaller minds to delicate tasks.

2 Prayer and good order *Read 1 Timothy 2*

Christian doctrine comes in nuggets in these letters, suddenly appearing in the midst of more practical instruction. So here verses 3–6 give a succinct statement of the heart of the gospel, couched in terms of Pauline breadth which much of the previous chapter belied.

The rest of the chapter, however, is concerned with church-centred issues. First, how shall we relate to the wider society? Certainly not by rocking the boat or agitating for social justice; rather, by taking our place as good pious citizens, alongside pagans and Jews, supporting the emperor with our prayers. It is a sharp contrast with aspects of the teaching of Jesus and shows for the first time Christian self-awareness as one element in a mixed society. It is a prototype of much that was to come (witness, for example, the State Prayers in the Book of Common Prayer). But was the theory adequate? What price martyrdom?

Solid convention wins again when it comes to church meetings. As in the synagogue, only men must pray and teach. Women, plain and unadorned, are to stay silent—all because of Eve's transgression. Here the writer uses (and elaborates) a piece of Jewish reflection on the story in Genesis 3. It seems to be his view that if (Christian) women rear children (to be recruits for the church?), they will escape the legacy of Eve.

Again Paul had transcended this level of thought. Christ as new Adam was the head and fount of a new human race, male and female alike (1 Corinthians 15:22, 45; Galatians 3:28). Even though in the creation story of Genesis 2 Eve had her origin in Adam, now in Christ, gender, as a fundamental distinction, was overcome. Women, sharing the Spirit, could pray and preach in Christian meetings (1 Corinthians 11:5), though they should not interrupt their husbands when it came to the man's turn (14:33–35); just as they might preside over a house-church (Romans 16:1, where 'deaconess' is a hopelessly anachronistic translation). On the whole, over the centuries the church has given much more weight to 1 Timothy than to Paul, so fitting in more smoothly with the way of the world. Pause for thought!

3 Standards for church leaders *Read 1 Timothy 3:1–15*

The writer turns to the structure of government that operates in the Christian communities known to him, and to the qualities it demands. Precisely what structure is in mind is not wholly clear, but we can make intelligent guesses. We begin by noting the reference to the church as a 'household' (in Greek, *oikos*) in verses 5 and 15. In the ancient world, that term signified something wider than the nuclear family of our day, including perhaps three generations, slaves and other dependants. It is no wonder that better-off households served as the bases for Christian communities once the movement established itself in the towns of Asia Minor, Greece and Italy. Converts gravitated towards the more substantial Christian houses for their meetings, and it would be natural for heads of households to preside at these gatherings for eucharist and prayer (see 1 Corinthians 11 and 14). Thus, the idea of the church as a family, God's family, has a long pedigree, whatever its different nuances.

It seems to have become customary to refer to these natural Christian leaders, perhaps several of them active in a particular city, as 'elders' (in Greek, *presbuteros*), an informal term for the natural 'seniors' in a given social setting. In due course it seems that, in a particular town, one among the 'elders' (a group we shall meet again later) assumed a leading role, perhaps not always with easy agreement. For such a one, the natural term was the ordinary word for 'supervisor' or 'warden' (in Greek, *episkopos*). And to help him, there emerged 'servants' or 'assistants' (in Greek, *diakonos*), who in due course became the main practical pastoral officers of the church. It is a matter of nice judgment when it becomes reasonable to translate these terms by the Christian technical terms, 'bishop' and 'deacon': not surely as early as this letter, written at a time when these arrangements were in their infancy and still fluid.

The qualities demanded of these Christian officers are serious and solid: temperance and modesty of character, experience in the faith and capacity to teach it are prime requirements—as is a good name in society at large (once again, we note that that wider dimension begins to be important for the church). They must be married (though, for no clear reason, not remarried), and must be male and reasonably well established socially. These criteria are in fact those for an ideal leader in the secular urban society of the Roman Empire. We miss the apostolic daring and enthusiasm of Paul, as also his sense of the Christian leader as reproducing Christ's pattern of self-giving and suffering. Here, for wholly understandable reasons, the mainstream of church life was being set on a path from which, in its ideals at least, it has not deviated—see the ordination services of any of the main churches.

4 Keeping the faith *Read 1 Timothy 3:16—4:16*

This section opens with the doctrinal centrepiece of the Pastoral Epistles, and it is a form of words unique in the New Testament. There is every likelihood that the passage beginning 'He was manifested...' is a sort of credal hymn current in the writer's circle. It may be that the explanation of the isolated character of the other doctrinal statements in these writings (e.g. 2:3–6) is that they too are set forms of words, perhaps familiar to both writer and readers. He appeals to them as fixed points in their spiritual universe. The RSV and other versions encourage us to see our passage in this way by printing it in six lines, like verse. Unlike other creed-like passages in the New Testament (for example, 1 Corinthians 15:3ff) and the creeds we use, this statement of faith does not lay out Christ's career in historical order, but places his earthly and heavenly roles in contrast, side by side. Thus, it refers to the former in lines 1, 4 and 5, and to the latter in lines 2, 3 (probably relating to Christ's victory over evil powers by the cross and then his heavenward journey) and 6. Like Philippians 2:6–11 and Colossians 1:15–20, this is a hymn concentrating wholly on Christ. With its Jewish background, early Christian faith could take for granted God as creator and sustainer of the world, and give its often ecstatic devotion to the new wonder of what Christ had done for us.

Having set out the core of belief in Christ, the writer returns to favourite territory: the need to fend off threats to true faith. It is a constant theme, sure sign of the difficulty in this early period of securing proper teaching authority in the church. He exerts all his efforts to making as sure as he can that the right people teach the right things. Making allowance for the polemical tone, we cannot be sure exactly what kind of people caused his anxiety. Their ascetic views (4:2)—later to be shared by many in the church's mainstream!—may indicate the sorts of people who emerged in the gnostic sects of the second century. The writer appeals robustly to belief in God as creator to refute these tendencies. There are also lesser points.

- *The writer 'flags up' some of his main points with the phrase 'the saying is sure', or 'trustworthy' (e.g. 4:9), indicating that these teachings are fundamental.*

- *Despite the strong sense of the enclosed (and embattled) Christian community, the vision of universal mission remains (4:10). And as we have seen, the war is not against society at large, more against dissidents close at hand and against evil spiritual powers.*

- *In 4:14, we have the earliest picture of the authorizing of Christian leaders, using the Jewish practice of the laying on of hands by the 'elders' (i.e. the men of 'weight'). It remains the practice at ordinations to this day, and here is its scriptural root.*

5 Care and maintenance *Read 1 Timothy 5*

This chapter seems to take up the theme of chapter 3, the attempt to legislate for particular groups in the Christian community. But now the accent shifts from leadership to welfare. Most of the chapter is about the care of widows, a particularly vulnerable group in the cities of the Greco-Roman world. Most men married women much younger than themselves, even in their early teens. As the age of death was commonly in the forties, women were often left at an early age with no obvious way of maintaining themselves and their offspring. The wider family might rally round, or a guild or friendly society might offer support. The Christian groups had something of the character of both. So we meet the earliest evidence of a formal church programme to care for its own needy members, a feature which was soon to become greatly extended. It was not long before it was the admiration of pagan neighbours: 'See how these Christians love one another' was the cry; Christianity worked in practice as well as theory. But we should be cautious. How many women survived to the age of sixty, given (as in modern Britain) as the age for qualifying for this localized old-age pension (v. 9)? Younger than that, they receive brisk advice—to remarry.

So perhaps it is a mistake to think, as some have done, of something like a formal order of enrolled widows playing a part in congregational life. But are 'the elders' more of an identifiable group, or (as suggested earlier and as outside evidence indicates) still a rather informal group—the men of weight, mostly on the older side (i.e. over thirty!), those whose counsel counts in the church's life? There are signs here that some of these people were beginning to be paid for their services (a move Paul resisted for himself in 1 Corinthians 9). Some (v. 17) are even worth double pay ('honour' is a euphemism; compare 'honorarium', like our use of 'a consideration'). It is beginning to be appropriate to translate *presbuteros* by a Christian technical term, 'presbyter' (as with 'bishop' in chapter 3).

6 Discipline for all *Read 1 Timothy 6*

The final part of the letter covers a miscellany of topics, all treated along lines that are now familiar. And incidentally, it is the source of a number of items of popular speech, some via the Book of Common Prayer: see verses 6, 7, 10, 12, 15, and also 5:23. The emphasis is on piety, modesty and seemly behaviour, which enter the repertoire of Christian qualities in these letters. The Greek words concerned—also common in Jewish and Greek moral teaching of the period—are virtually confined to these letters as far as the New Testament is concerned. We notice once more subtle modifications of Paul's teaching. For instance, compare verse 2 with Paul's 'there is neither slave nor free' (Galatians 3:28). And Christ's passion is described in terms of his courage and fidelity to the truth (v. 13), i.e. not doctrinally but morally. Sobriety of life is the dominant note, and we get a picture of the urban Christian communities envisaged here as centring on people of moderate wealth, neither rich nor poor, and ready to be generous.

The most intriguing passage is verse 20. The exhortation is of course typical, but interest focuses on the word translated 'contradictions'. The Greek is *antitheseis*, which was the title of the chief work of Marcion, one of the leading heretics of the first half of the second century. He rejected the Jewish roots of Christianity, including the old scriptures, which he saw as presenting a deity far removed from the God and Father of Jesus; and (quite unfairly) he reckoned Paul as the patron of his teaching. It has been suggested that our writer, working as if in the time of Paul and in his name, is here subtly urging rejection of Marcion's doctrine: he himself is Paul's true heir. If there were anything in this suggestion, it would date the Pastoral Epistles as late as the second quarter of the second century. Others have had the same idea on the grounds of similarities to the writings of Polycarp, bishop of Smyrna at that time. It is also the case, for what it is worth, that the Pastorals are absent from the earliest surviving copy of Paul's letters (Papyrus 46), dating from about AD200. Whatever its origin, 'guard the deposit' is a slogan often invoked in defence of faithfulness to tradition.

GUIDELINES

The general exhortation to show respect to Christian leaders in 1 Timothy is an example of the hierarchical frame of mind that dominated the society of the time, whether pagan or Jewish. All decent people would have applauded. We miss the Christ-centred, often radical note which sounds through Paul's exhortations to leaders and others. Are Christian leaders (not to mention Christians in general!) always liable to adopt the colour of the surrounding culture? How admirable is that?

11–17 MAY — 2 TIMOTHY AND TITUS

1 The perspective of faith *Read 2 Timothy 1*

We are by now familiar with the leading ideas and attitudes of our writer, and we can pause to notice aspects so far neglected. For example, these writings did more than others in the New Testament to establish the word 'saviour' as a term to describe Jesus (v. 10), as indeed also God himself. As Matthew 1:21 indicates, this meaning is present in the Jewish name, Joshua, of which 'Jesus' is the Greek equivalent. The idea of Jesus as the agent of our rescue from enemies ranging from Satan to death and sin is well established in early Christian writings, from Paul onwards; and with the rescue come the gifts of 'life and immortality'. In the first century, when life was generally brief, immortality was given high value, and its prominence in the Christian message was of major importance.

But in the Christian scheme, a more precise objective was in view—the time referred to in verses 12 and 18 simply as 'that day', when Christ would return and the whole world order would be judged and renewed by God's power, with the gift of eternal bliss for his chosen ones. For good or ill, in recent years many Christians have lost this perspective, which without doubt dominated Christian minds and hearts in the early days. Despite the strong concern in these letters with this-worldly matters, the conviction of a not-far-distant consummation remains. It is very different from the modern expectation that if a faith is to be relevant, it must speak above all to the problems of social and personal life here and now. The apocalyptic imagery prevalent in the Christian imagination of the first century (and of later ages) may not now speak to anything like all Christians, let alone people in general. But did it embody a sense of transcendent power and wonder without which religion is crippled?

2 Timothy's work *Read 2 Timothy 2*

This chapter, together with chapter 4, puts the greatest strain on the prevailing scholarly view that the Pastorals are not by Paul: here is so much personal detail that pure invention seems to be ruled out. Yet, as has been said, such writing is far from lacking parallels in the period, and most of the themes here in 2 Timothy occur elsewhere in the Pastorals. Moreover, 1 Timothy and Titus do not lack personal and geographical references, as well as what we can call 'skewed' reminiscences of Paul's undoubted works. We have met a number of examples. In this chapter, such parallels are close, for example verse 5 with 1 Corinthians 9:24, verse 8 with Romans 1:3. It is hard to know whether such parallels are likely to be imitations or Paul's own repetitions of favourite ideas. More significant, here alone we have in verses 9–12 a theme otherwise absent from the Pastorals but central to Paul's sense of himself as Christ's missionary: readiness to suffer as he did. Such matters justify the view that 2 Timothy has more claim to be truly Paul's than do the other two writings.

There is, however, something of a difficulty over the figure of Timothy himself. How are we to understand his persona in these writings? He is a Christian leader, but the writer depicts him as young (1 Timothy 4:12; 2 Timothy 2:22), which, in the world of the first century, implies late teens or early twenties. A sceptic might feel that (on the basis of Acts 16:1–3?) the writer has frozen Timothy, Peter Pan-like, at an early age, his role here being simply that of the authentic bearer of the Pauline tradition. So it may be, but in a society where age was the passport to respect, the depiction is puzzling; and 1 Timothy 4:12 suggests that not everybody would agree with the role cast for him. What is plain is that the writer enjoins on responsible figures in the church the highest degree of fidelity to the gospel and goodness of life.

3 Dark times ahead *Read 2 Timothy 3*

The writer now lets his imagination range freely in a way that was quite common both in early Christianity and in other circles, pagan and especially Jewish. The world was running down and before the final catastrophe there would be unprecedented outbreaks of wickedness and hostility to God's faithful people. The long list of forms of misbehaviour (vv. 2ff) is conventional but nevertheless bloodcurdling. Among the conventions is the particular vulnerability of women in such circumstances (see 1 Timothy 2:14). We are confirmed in the impression that the writer's culture is at least partly Jewish by the reference to Jannes and Jambres, the legendary (post-scriptural) names for the wizards of Egypt who resisted Moses in the run-up to the Exodus. The writer claims his own share of sufferings for the gospel: verse 11 refers to matters recorded in Acts 13–14.

The essentially Jewish background is evident in the appeal to the scriptures as support and instructor, though, interestingly, they are never formally quoted. The reference is to (essentially) what we know as the Old Testament. These writings were receiving official recognition in Judaism as a collection towards the end of the first century, in effect ratifying their already customary use. Christians had inherited them, and they read them as foreshadowing and testifying to Christ as their fulfilment. Their wider instructional role remained, though, and its precise form and limits caused much debate, as indeed from time to time throughout Christian history. Books of Christian provenance (the New Testament) acquired the same canonical status in the course of the second century, though some were already seen as having authority: witness our own writer's readiness to lean on the letters of Paul. This passage is the clearest warrant for the doctrine of the inspiration of scripture and has commonly been applied, out of context, to the whole Bible—which did not yet exist.

4 Words of affection *Read 2 Timothy 4*

The final chapter of this letter is much the most moving part of the Pastoral Epistles. It is warm and direct, giving a clear sense of the intimacy of the Christian network in the early period, even across distances of time and space. It is all the more poignant in that Paul has been shown writing from prison (1:8), and, if the letter is genuinely Paul's work, then this letter shares that origin with Philippians, Colossians, Philemon and (though there is again doubt about its authenticity) Ephesians.

It is in this passage indeed that the authenticity of at least 2 Timothy among the Pastorals or, at any rate, of this and the other more personal parts of 2 Timothy, is hardest to doubt. In recent years at least two highly reputable scholars have proposed that this letter is indeed by Paul, and they have suggested how it might fit into his career.

The opening verses especially have an urgency and sense of anxiety that moves many readers. It is a protest not only against error but also against superficiality and frivolity in religion, the love of novelty for novelty's sake. In such circumstances, the Christian leader and teacher must hold on at all cost, secure in hope of the coming deliverance. It is the same message as that in the speech of Paul to the Ephesian elders in Acts 20 (especially vv. 29–31), the only speech in Acts delivered to a

Christian audience. (This similarity, among others, has prompted some to see Luke, the author of Acts, as involved also in the writing of these letters.) Resolute rejection of deviance is of course a note struck time and again in these letters, always without any full or clear statement of precisely what teaching is being opposed. We simply cannot tell whether this is religious speculation of Jewish or pagan origin—or indeed how far it is right to distinguish rigorously between the two. For his part, the writer maintains the eschatological hope of Christianity from its beginning: 'the day' is near.

The names are mostly known from either Acts or Paul's undoubted letters, testifying either to authenticity or to efficient scene-setting. The whole chapter follows the conventions of its type of composition, 'the prison-letter'; but then, what else would one expect such a one to write?

5 High standards for all *Read Titus 1–2*

Titus, like Timothy, is known from his appearances in the Corinthians letters of Paul as one of his leading assistants. The contents of this letter addressed to him are broadly similar to those of 1 Timothy. On the theory that all three letters were composed together by a devotee of Paul in the years following his lifetime, there is something to be said for the idea that they were planned as a sort of triptych. The two outer panels cover roughly the same ground—relating to leadership in the church and the danger from heresy. These two themes come together in the positive aim of standing firm on the true faith of the gospel. The central panel differs in concerning itself more with personal matters.

Nevertheless, careful reading reveals differences between 1 Timothy and Titus, notably in the arrangement of church leadership. In 1 Timothy 3, the picture is of a single 'overseer' ('bishop'), assisted by 'servants' ('deacons'), working alongside 'elders' ('presbyters'). Here, however, the first and last of these categories seem blurred, as if they may be two angles on the same roles, referring respectively to task and status. That way of looking at the matter confirms the idea that these writings reflect a stage when the single Christian leader in a town was only just emerging from the group of natural leaders, probably the heads of the more substantial Christian households, each the focus of its own Christian group or house-church.

As in 1 Timothy 6:9–10, this letter takes up the common early Christian hostility to money-grubbing (1:11), a vice attributed to opponents (in this case, Jews). The question of attitudes to money—its necessity but its many pitfalls—attracts a good deal of attention from early Christian writers, ranging from Jesus' own prescription for the shedding of property (Mark 1: 16–20; 10:29) and praise of the poor (Luke 6:20) to the more complex problems encountered once the Christian movement was established in towns and needed some wealth in order to survive (1 Corinthians 9; James 1–2).

The only other evidence for a Christian relationship with Crete (1:5) comes from Acts 27: Paul and company moored there en route to Rome. Verse 12 hardly contributes to good local relations. It has also given logicians a well-known teaser: if the Cretan prophet says all Cretans are liars, can you believe him?

6 The Christians' image *Read Titus 3*

In 1 Timothy 2 we met an early example of Christian attempts to come to terms peaceably with the secular society in which the church finds itself. Here, in the opening verses of this chapter, the writer reverts to the same topic, enjoining obedience to accredited authorities. Paul had already given the same advice in Romans 13, and we recall the story of the tribute money in Mark 12:13–17. Through most of Christian history this policy has prevailed. But there have been many occasions when it has seemed to fly in the face of more fundamental Christian duties—for example, to stand against cruelty and injustice and to preserve the right to worship and to teach the faith when governments seek to suppress it. The line taken here comes from a time when the church was so small and obscure that problems arose only rarely; but Christians in Rome had already been made scapegoats for a disastrous fire and their firmness against emperor-worship would soon be noticed and held against them, sometimes with martyrdom as the outcome. Has this writer partly got his eye on such hostility, claiming that Christians are sober citizens who are no danger to civil peace? They have positively forsaken all vice and antisocial behaviour, because of their commitment to Christ.

In describing this transformation, the writer makes his one reference to baptism, as the rite of entry to Christian commitment. He calls it a 'washing of rebirth', a radical image, found also in John 3 and 1 Peter 3. It is the entry to a whole new life.

GUIDELINES

Readers may have felt that the spiritual content of these notes has been on the meagre side. Partly, there has been need of a good deal of explanatory material to make the context of the letters as clear as possible. But it is also a matter of the content of these writings themselves. Few would feel that, apart from a few passages, they approach the level of religious intensity to be found in the Gospels, the undoubted letters of Paul and indeed in most of the other New Testament writings. Indeed their very title, 'The Pastoral Epistles', points to their concern being chiefly with practical matters: how the shepherding of God's people should be arranged and their welfare catered for, how they should be protected against spiritual dangers and encouraged to stick to their beliefs in the face of threats and subversion.

So the deepest challenge they make to us is perhaps the need to discern the spiritual in the humdrum, the hand of God in the affairs of every day. Of course, as we have seen, the Pastorals do not lack some passages that do just that, and they are always to the point. It is simply that, not doubting the solid faith and genuine Christian perception that they show, we may feel a certain lack of integration of these passages with those that are more practical. After all, Paul managed to see that the spirit of the gospel penetrated right to the heart of his dealings with the most mundane situations. Do we nowadays sustain the level of spirituality even of the Pastoral Epistles? What are our essential 'nuggets' of faith?

Further reading

J.L. Houlden, *The Pastoral Epistles*, SCM Press, and Margaret Davies, *The Pastoral Epistles*, Epworth Press, are two recent accessible commentaries.

Stephen G. Wilson, *Luke and the Pastoral Epistles*, SPCK, and Michael Prior, *Paul the Letter-Writer and the Second Letter to Timothy*, Sheffield Academic Press, explore particular aspects of the Pastorals.

Judges 1–8

The book of Judges is not one of the easiest books of the Bible for twentieth-century consciences to read. It is not simply that it contains ruthless, barbaric and harrowing scenes, but that the author obviously has no qualms about making God the perpetrator of much of the violence he portrays and that those who decided that his book should be sacred scripture had no qualms either. We can, of course, deal with this at one level by simply reminding ourselves that here is an ancient book, author and religious community whose values are different from ours; and if we remember that, there is much that we can read in Judges with profit. But our problem goes deeper. It concerns not only the morality of Judges but also its theology. The backbone of the book is the doctrine that goodness is rewarded and evil is punished and we know, just as other parts of the Bible also recognize, that this theology does not work in real life where the bad prosper and the good suffer every bit as much as the other way round. Nonetheless this is a powerful theology and its lasting legacy is known to everyone who has been faced with the agonized and often accusatory, 'What have I done to deserve this?' So a major difficulty in reading the book of Judges is that it focuses, maybe more clearly than anywhere else, the moral and theological problems of reading the Bible in the late twentieth century. It makes us ask: how can we say 'This is the Word of the Lord' after readings such as these?

The version used is the New Revised Standard Version.

18–24 MAY — JUDGES 1:1—3:11

1 After the death of Joshua *Read Judges 1:1–15*

We join a long story partway through. In the Hebrew Bible, Joshua–Kings tells the story of Israel from a bright beginning on the wrong side of the River Jordan, into the Promised Land and then away to exile in Babylon. Its moral is simple—Israel is

God's people and the tragedy is that they have brought the catastrophe of the exile on themselves by disobedience and wrongdoing. The story so far is that the Israelites have crossed the Jordan and conquered their way into the Promised Land. Canaanites a-plenty remain, stubbornly defending their homeland and preventing the Israelites from occupying it completely.

Verse 1 sets the scene and reveals the theme of the book. The great Joshua is dead and the Israelites faithfully 'inquire of the Lord' about how his leadership is to be continued. Here is a picture of complete faithfulness. They know that they depend entirely on God and that they must look to him alone for their security. The following verses illustrate that such real faithfulness is rewarded by real blessings. The remaining Canaanites will not stand a chance.

The Israelites appear as a loosely organized group of tribes who sometimes pull together and sometimes act independently. In verse 2 Judah is singled out and, as the larger story unfolds in Samuel and Kings, this tribe proves to be the most faithful of them all, though even Judah's story will end in tears. In verse 4 we meet the first enemy alliance. It is defeated. With hardly a murmur Adoni-Bezek ('The Lord of Bezek') recognizes that he has got his just deserts and that God has paid him back in his own coin (v. 7; compare Matthew 7:2). Verse 8 hints that this will happen to Israel too, though it will take them centuries to get the message; for as the Judahites capture and destroy Jerusalem so later will the Babylonians (2 Kings 24–25). Verse 12 introduces us to a feature we will meet again—rash promises and their consequences. This one is fine. Others will not be.

2 An incomplete victory *Read Judges 1:16–28*

Next to its genealogies the names of peoples and places in passages like this are among the Bible's most formidable deterrents to an easy read. Many commentaries fill pages with attempts at identification, but we must ignore many of them here if we want to see the wood for the trees.

The tribes of Judah, Simeon and possibly Manasseh are portrayed as individuals ('He went' etc), Benjamin is referred to as 'the Benjaminites' ('the sons of Benjamin') and Joseph as 'the house of Joseph'. Are these different ways of referring to these brother tribes preparing us for some of the later disagreements between them? There were also smaller groups which belonged to this emerging nation (v. 16). The reality was more complicated than the traditional family tree of the 'twelve tribes' suggests.

The 'city of palms' in verse 16 is Jericho (see 2 Chronicles 28:15).

Verse 17 tells of a city being 'put to the ban', totally destroyed as an offering to God. The Hebrew word for the practice is *herem*, hence the renaming of the site as 'Hormah'—'Destroyed in Dedication to God'.

Verse 18 presents a problem. These are three of the five Philistine cities, and the Philistines appear later as Israel's most powerful enemy which is not subdued until the time of David. The Greek version of this verse reflects that and says that Judah did *not* capture these cities—supported by verse 19. However, GNB is the only modern version to follow this interpretation, though others refer to it in the margin.

There is confusion also over the fate of Jerusalem; taken by Judah in verse 8 but back in Jebusite hands in verse 21 where it remains until David captures it (2 Samuel 5:6–10).

'To this day' (vv. 21 and 26) occurs over thirty times in our longer story, often in explanations of customs or place names. In verse 26 it reinforces the point that the consequences of obedience or disobedience are real and lasting. We might deduce from verse 21 that the writer was at work before David's capture of Jerusalem, but few scholars do.

Verses 27–28 begin to sound warning notes. Here are continuing Canaanites, and the most that Israel can do is enslave them. In the light of Deuteronomy 11:8, what is going on?

3 From 'Rolling Stones' to 'Weepers' *Read Judges 1:29—2:5*

The worrying trend continues. The Israelites may subjugate the Canaanites but they cannot evict them and in the case of one group of Amorites they cannot do even that (v. 34). The Amorites, occupying territory in the north of the region and east of the Jordan, are the third major ethnic group to appear in these chapters following the Philistines in the coastal plain and the Canaanites everywhere else. The other names in chapter 1 are of inhabitants of towns or areas, though the Perizzites and the 'three sons (clans) of Anak' might be small ethnic groups and verse 36 should probably read 'the border of the Edomites' rather than '...the Amorites'.

The 'angel of the Lord' brings the truth home to them in a salutary way (vv. 1–5). He comes from Gilgal, the place where Joshua had set up the memorial stones celebrating God's help when his people first crossed the Jordan (see Joshua 4:19–24 and 5:9). 'Angels' in the Old Testament are usually members of the 'heavenly host' sent to deliver a message, but they can be human 'messengers' such as prophets. We will look at them again in connection with Judges 6. As there is no sign of anyone being terrified by his appearance, this angel may be one of the latter variety. This messenger, divine or human, speaks in the name of God and in language and style reminiscent of Joshua 24, but here his words are a dire warning that the consequences of their failure to drive out the Canaanites will not be peaceful coexistence but conflict and temptation. In contrast to Gilgal they will now see the Lord's power used against his people rather than for them. The place of this message is not named 'Bochim' ('Weepers') for nothing. They might weep but it won't change things; the die is cast.

Our problem here is obvious. Anyone who went around today saying that the troubles in modern Israel are due to its failure to rid itself of the land's indigenous Arab population would quite rightly be seen as a dangerous fanatic. But that is clearly what our author believes. To put it bluntly, his God demands ethnic cleansing but our God prefers peaceful coexistence in a multi-faith, multi-cultural and multi-ethnic world. There are conflicting values here.

4 True and false allegiance *Read Judges 2:6–15*

All the main themes of Judges are found in 2:6—3:11. Verses 6–10a are an expansion of Joshua 24:29–30 and review the failure of the Israelites so far. With Joshua and his generation, all had been well. Not so with the next generation. Verses 11–15 preview how the sad story will continue. The issue is allegiance to the Lord.

Verses 6–10 give three illustrations of how Joshua and his generation had prospered because they had given true allegiance to the Lord: everyone had taken possession of their inheritances, Joshua had lived to a great age and the whole generation had died in peace. To be 'gathered to their ancestors' is not a reference to life after death. This idea was unknown in Israel until later and was still controversial at the time of Jesus. It means to die a good death in old age rather than an untimely one. Here this expression is used about a large number of people; elsewhere it is only used about the deaths of the great heroes Abraham, Isaac, Jacob, Moses and Josiah. It and the 'Moreover…' emphasize how faithful this whole generation has been. Giving true allegiance to the Lord ('knowing the Lord') is demonstrated by recognizing what he has done and by worshipping only him.

Verses 11–15 tell a different story. The Israelites of the next generation suffer because they fail to give true allegiance to the Lord. Their inheritance is plundered, their enemies overcome them and every battle ends in defeat. They do not recognize what he has done and abandon him to worship Baal (or the Baals) and the Astartes (or the Ashtoreths or the Ashtaroth). Baal—'Lord' or 'Master'—is used in the plural or without a capital letter to refer to local gods (as in verse 11); but Baal was also the name of the Canaanite high god (as in verse 13). Astarte (the Greek form of her name) or Ashtaroth (the Hebrew form) was one of the three chief Canaanite goddesses, her speciality being love and fertility. In the plural and without capital letters the word refers to local 'goddesses'. Although ancient and modern translations get quite muddled, in both cases the picture is plain enough: Israel is guilty of apostasy and the consequences are devastating.

5 The 'Judges' *Read Judges 2:16–23*

In this passage we see God's frustration. The long story so far is that he has saved the Israelites from Egypt (the Exodus etc), given them good advice for living in their new freedom (the Ten Commandments etc) and helped them into the Promised Land. But his generosity is rewarded by betrayal. And no sooner does he rescue them from the consequences of their misdeeds than they do it all over again. He feels both pity (v. 18) and anger (v. 20). Whatever we make of these emotions, they show that God is not remote from or indifferent to his world and his people but passionately involved with both.

God takes the initiative in rescuing his people by 'raising up judges' ('leaders' GNB, 'chieftains' NJPS)—the characters who give our book its title. This is a rather misleading term for these people, for most of them are charismatic heroes rather than having any legal standing, guerrilla leaders with a local or temporary mission, though there are some who seem to have a responsibility for administering justice (Judges 4:4, 10:1–5 and 12:7–15).

Note the variety of expressions for Israel's faithfulness and unfaithfulness, one of the main ones being that of 'walking' (vv. 17 and 22). Faith in God involves making choices (to go this way or that? to do this or that?) and decisions (about belief, behaviour, values). The possibility of 'walking' in other 'ways' than those offered by the God who has made himself known to them is to be their real test (vv. 22–23).

6 Faithfulness is tested *Read Judges 3:1–11*

How the Israelites moved from believing that the Lord was the only God for them to their final view that he is the only God there is (as in Isaiah 40—55) is a long and complicated story. In this passage, set in an age of many gods, the test for Israel is to give its exclusive allegiance to only one of them, the Lord, the God who had brought them out of Egypt. Some scholars see other reasons for this insistence on loyalty to the Lord alone, such as that the worship of the other local gods included immoral sexual acts or that these other religions condoned or promoted social structures which exploited the poor. They insist that the way of the Lord involved a commitment to moral values and a vision of social justice which could not be compromised.

That may be so or it may not, but exclusive allegiance to the Lord is a test which Israel fails. In verses 6–7 intermarriage is seen as both the cause and the example of such failure (cf. 1 Kings 11:1–8; Ezra 9:1–2). *Asherah* is the main Canaanite goddess (e.g. 1 Kings 18:19) and *asherim* (the Hebrew masculine plural) are sacred poles or trees erected as her symbols (e.g. Deuteronomy 12:3). Verse 7 is the only place where the feminine plural is used (the *Asherahs* or *Asheroth*).

With Othniel we meet the first of these charismatic leaders, empowered by God's spirit and thereby victorious. Verse 10 is a good example of the Old Testament's understanding of the 'spirit of the Lord' as God's dynamic power given to someone to empower them for a specific task. I do hope the name Cushan-rishathaim of Aram-naharaim is not the awful play on words (Cushan Double-Trouble of Aram of the Two Rivers) that my NRSV footnote says it is.

GUIDELINES

The longer story of which Judges is a part probably began originally with Deuteronomy and so we usually call the one who wove it all together the 'Deuteronomic Historian'. The NRSV follows ancient Christian tradition and calls Joshua–Esther 'The Historical Books'. This can be misleading unless we remember that this history, like all history ancient or modern, is not straight reporting but has a message to convey.

Ideas about the early days of Israel are complex and controversial. For some scholars the Bible story tells it the way it was, beginning with Abraham and getting clearer as it goes. Others are much more cautious. What is increasingly widely agreed is that Israel as a people and an embryo nation came on the scene ('emerged' is the favourite word) around 1200BC. Major population growth, changes in the settlement patterns in the central highlands of Canaan around this time and accompanying social upheaval in the older city states in the region, which the historians observe, are not very different from the way the story is told in Judges.

The NRSV calls the book of Judges 'the story of a new community emerging from disparate groups that were trying to create an entirely new pattern of life... one in which all citizens had an equal range of opportunities. The Israelites rejected the absolutism of the Canaanite city states with their oppressive political and social systems... the creation of this new society was an immense struggle. In the midst of revolutionary social upheaval, the Israelites found support in their belief that they were ruled by the Lord who took the side of the lowly against their oppressors.'

Whatever difficulties we may have with the ethics or theology of Judges, this way of reading it gives us a powerful message for church and society today. It also gives renewed urgency to our prayers that God's kingdom will come and his will be done on earth as in heaven.

25–31 MAY — JUDGES 3:12—5:31

1 Ehud son of Gera *Read Judges 3:12–31*

Here are tales of wit, cunning and strength. The story of Ehud has a fine cast of characters (a fat enemy king, a left-handed hero, non-plussed servants) and a witty plot. The note about Shamgar and the Philistines (a trailer for the longer story of Samson) may only be short, but it packs a real punch—six hundred Philistine infantrymen equipped with the latest weaponry (remember 1:19) defeated by one Israelite with a homemade farm implement. An ox-goad was a light wooden pole about eight feet long with a small iron spike at one end with which to tap your ox and a small blade at the other for cleaning your plough.

There is another character in the Ehud story. It is the Lord, who fattened up King Eglon (v. 12), raised up Ehud (v. 15) and finally gave the Moabites into the hands of the Israelite militia (v. 28). He is a character who makes things happen. But reading the story like this causes problems for some who read it today. Does it mean that we must accept a God who acts in our world, who intervenes now to punish or to bless, who controls our history? Many Christians say 'yes' and point to signs of his activity today. Others say 'no'. They see rampant injustice, suffering and death and can only explain this by dispensing with an intervening God. If such a god exists, they say, and doesn't act or intervene, then he doesn't deserve to be called God at all. These are serious questions, perhaps the most serious questions of all, but they overlook three basic points. They overlook the fact that we have been reading a story; that the world in the story is not the same as the one we live in and that stories can be good stories which fire our imaginations, nerve our souls or change our ways with all sorts of odd characters and unlikely events in them.

The Ehud story has six parts, most of which recur in standard form in all the stories of the judges which follow: Israel does 'what was evil in the sight of the Lord'; God delivers them into the hands of an enemy; they cry for help; God sends them help; the enemy is defeated and the land 'has rest' for a period.

2 Deborah the prophetess *Read Judges 4:1–10*

The cycle begins again. Israel 'does what is evil in the sight of the Lord' (v. 1). What that is exactly is not specified, but the fact that 'the Lord' is mentioned three times in three verses is enough to show that true or false allegiance is again the issue (as at 3:7). The 'Lord', written in capitals in most translations, represents the not-to-be-pronounced personal name written as 'Yahweh' in the New Jerusalem Bible. A major question in Judges is, simply: who is to be Israel's God? The writer's conviction is that it can only be the Lord, as we see in the titles added to his name so far: 'the God of your ancestors' (2:12), 'your God' (3:7) and 'the God of Israel' (4:6). This time the oppressor comes from the north.

Women in positions of authority are few and far between in

the Old Testament, and of them Deborah, a prophetess who 'judges' all Israel, is second only to Miriam, Moses' sister (Exodus 15:20). Five female Israelite prophetesses are mentioned in the Old Testament and four of them are named—Miriam herself, Huldah in 2 Kings 22:14, Noadiah in Nehemiah 6:14 (who was a dubious one) and Isaiah's wife in Isaiah 8:3. Verse 4 refers to Deborah as 'a' prophetess rather than 'the' prophetess, maybe indicating that the phenomenon of a woman in this role was not as unusual as the scarcity of their names and appearance in the Old Testament might suggest. In addition to being a prophetess Deborah is one of those 'judges' who had an established role. Her responsibility in administering justice was widely known and used (v. 5). There is also no mention of her being empowered by God's spirit to undertake the task she is given to do. She summons Barak and she speaks to him with all the authority a prophet has as the messenger of God.

Often in call stories there is a note of reluctance, and Barak exercises that prerogative here. He will only go if Deborah goes with him. Deborah agrees, but the price he pays for his hesitation is that a woman (no mention yet of which one) will get the credit for the victory. He calls the militia from two of the northern tribes, and no doubt their numbers are as exaggerated as those of Sisera's chariotry.

3 Jael and the tent-peg *Read Judges 4:11–24*

Quite how many fathers-in-law Moses had is an interesting question. Three names are mentioned: Reuel, the priest of Midian (Exodus 2:18–22), Jethro, the priest of Midian (Exodus 3:1) and Hobab the Kenite (Judges 1:16). As Reuel and Jethro are both referred to as Zipporah's father, they must be the same person, as in all likelihood is Hobab. Just to complicate matters, Hobab's father is called Reuel in the Numbers passage, where he is also shown to be a Midianite.

We see from these references that Jethro first appears in the exodus and settlement stories at the key point where Moses is commissioned to lead the Lord's people out of Egypt, and Hobab first appears as a guide to lead the Israelites through the desert to Mount Sinai. The special relationship between the Kenites (possibly a sub-group of the Midianites and usually regarded as a tribe of wandering smiths) and the Israelites is seen again in this passage and later on in 1 Samuel 15:6. Here their appearance introduces the story of how another woman, Jael, brings victory to the Lord. Notice how this passage in a book of heroes highlights Israel's dependence on foreigners and women.

It is God who fights the battle (vv. 14, 15 and 23)—'because there is none other that fighteth for us, but only thou O God'—a theme which is taken up in the song in the next chapter. The battle takes place on the plain of Jezreel, which puts Israel at even more of a disadvantage against Sisera's massed chariots. Most translations talk about the Lord throwing the Canaanites 'into a panic' at verse 15; only NIV follows the Hebrew, which has the Lord throwing them down before the sword.

Deborah's gift of looking into the future (remember that you could go to prophets to ask them to use that power just to look around for your lost asses—1 Samuel 9:5–10) is shown to be accurate. In a simple tale we read how her words were proved true. Jael greets Barak at her tent door with the announcement that the man he is seeking is inside. Dead.

4 The Song of Deborah and Barak (1) *Read Judges 5:1–9*

This song is probably the oldest part of the Hebrew Bible and the oldest Israelite poem in existence. The meaning of this victory song is obvious, but much of the detail is so obscure that the translations vary enormously.

NRSV keeps the reference to long hair in verse 2. It is a sign of dedication to God, as with the Nazirites (Numbers 6:5) and Samson. Most other translations have leaders offering leadership and people willingly following. NJB combines both possibilities.

To 'bless the Lord' is much more than to praise or thank him; it is to affirm, acknowledge and acclaim him. In verses 2 and 9 the Lord is acclaimed as the victorious God; later in the Old Testament as the true and only God. Hence the response,

'Thanks be to God' to the call 'Let us bless the Lord' is very weak, and a much better response would be, 'We will sing his praise and exalt him for ever' or the people's cry in 1 Kings 18:39.

Verses 4–5 are a good example of 'theophany' language which speaks of the Lord appearing in a terrifying storm (see Exodus 19:16–20 and Psalm 97:1–5). But note that in the other famous story about Elijah, God is no longer found in the earthquake, wind and fire (1 Kings 19:11–12). Seir (possibly another mountain), Edom and Sinai are all dry and desert south-eastern places, and anyone who has experienced a desert storm knows the devastating power in this picture. It is a terrifying sight to see this desert God, the Lord, marching on to war (see also Deuteronomy 33:1–5).

The victory is God's, but the poem still celebrates the contribution made to that victory by others, especially Deborah in verses 6–9 and Jael in verses 24–27. The first part of verse 7 is difficult. NRSV talks about prosperous peasants enjoying the new life which was born with Deborah's leadership. Other translations agree that she brought to birth a wonderful change, but see verse 7 as describing the barrenness and hardship that existed before she came on the scene. Verses 8–9 emphasize the impossibility of the task she faced and the amazing result she achieved. So many people had gone after new gods that there was no one left to fight for the true God until Deborah took the lead.

5 The Song of Deborah and Barak (2) *Read Judges 5:10–21*

In verses 10–11, rich (those who ride on top-of-the-range asses) and poor (those who walk) alike are invited to join in the song of the Lord's victories or 'righteous acts' (AV). The AV is helpful here as long as we remember that in the Old Testament 'righteousness' is a warm and positive word. A righteous person is someone who takes action to put things right. Used about God it indicates that he takes the initiative in putting wrong things right again. That sense is clear here and made even clearer when translated as 'gracious acts'.

The call to Deborah and Barak to 'awake' and 'arise' in verse 12 is not a matter of rousing them to action but of celebrating their certainty of victory because the army is 'marching in the power of God'. Although more tribes are mentioned in the song than in the prose version in chapter 4, it was still a David and Goliath sort of contest (v. 13). The song celebrates the heroism of the tribes which responded to the call, singling out Zebulun and Naphtali who were the only tribes taking part in the prose version (v. 18). It also harangues others for not joining in who were never invited in the prose version. Machir was the son of Manasseh (Joshua 17:1) and that name in verse 14 stands for either the whole tribe of Manasseh or a significant part of it.

The army of Israel marches to battle only to see the enemy defeated by the mighty power of God (vv. 19–21). Heaven and earth combine as his weapons and the Canaanites are defeated. The vivid metaphor of fighting stars is found only here in the Old Testament but there are parallels in various ancient Mesopotamian texts. There is no need to resort to such prosaic explanations as chariots getting bogged down in the mud.

At this point, just as she had in verse 9, the singer interrupts the poem with a shout which can't be held back ('March on, my soul, with might') because she is so caught up with emotion at this great victory. But why 'she'? And why does tradition and the NRSV call this song the 'Song of Deborah' when according to verse 1 it was a duet?

6 The Song of Deborah and Barak (3) *Read Judges 5:22–31*

The battle may have been fought and won by the Lord, but that does not excuse the nearby villagers of Meroz for staying at home (v. 23). He might not have needed their help, but they were not to know that and at least it should have been offered. Their curse is contrasted by the richest blessing upon Jael for what she did to help (vv. 24–27). Only a woman, and a 'tent-dwelling' foreign woman at that, Jael gave help where it was needed, first to Sisera and then to the Lord. The sacred laws of hospitality are honoured and then broken, though the song gives us no clue to her motives. The Merozites had every reason to help the Lord and didn't; she had every reason not to and did.

The final scene in verses 28–30 introduces a third woman, Sisera's mother. Any sympathy we may feel for this mother's pain in verse 28 is dissipated by her callous indifference in verse 30 to the feelings of other women, let alone that of their mothers or their men. Nonetheless, here is the first picture in Judges of an innocent victim. She is not named, but she is at least described and her suffering acknowledged. Amid all its glorying in war, with hosts of slain scattered all over the place, here and in one other place (11:34–40) Judges hints that there is another side to this violence. It is the price paid by women, the mothers or the daughters of these heroes.

As the singer had introduced the song and twice interrupted it, so she concludes it. Hers is a simple world of good and bad. And so is the writer's. He simply adds his concluding note to this particular cycle. Once more, his point has been made and illustrated.

GUIDELINES

Much of this week we have been reading what is by anyone's standards a most magnificent poem. Yet it is one which for many expresses the most dreadful and unacceptable of sentiments.

What, as praying and worshipping people, are we to make of these pictures of a 'Lord of battles, God of armies'? Parts of the church today are very reluctant to sing hymns like 'Onward Christian soldiers, marching as to war' or to use any sort of language which suggests that the church or its God is militant here on earth. At the same time other parts of the church in the West will sing quite happily about God 'building a people of power' and see this reluctance as a sign of weakness and lack of faith. In some other parts of the world our Christian brothers and sisters would say that if God is not actively campaigning on the part of the poor and the marginalized then he is not the God of the Bible, and that any church which is not campaigning in that way is not the Church of the Christ who was and is the champion of the poor.

In all of this we can see how much we are all shaped by the values of the world we live in and of the place we occupy in that world, and of how different all our modern worlds are from the world of the song of Deborah and Barak.

It may be that those of us who are less 'militant' need to be gripped by the passion and commitment of this song. For it is quite clear that in the Old Testament's stories of true and false allegiance much more is at stake than the Lord's personal reputation. The Elijah stories, which we have mentioned a couple of times this week, show that one of the things at stake, in the question of who was God in Israel, was that set of moral values and community standards in which justice, care for the weak and love of neighbour were important. Other gods did not share that vision and demand that ethical commitment, or so the Deuteronomic Historian believed. So acknowledging that the Lord is God means joining a battle for the cause of 'justice, peace and the integrity of creation'.

Perhaps, therefore, imagery about fighting the good fight should have some place in the mission of God's people today? If so, those who are doing it need a place in our prayers.

1–7 JUNE — JUDGES 6:1—8:35

1 A prophet, the angel and Gideon *Read Judges 6:1–18*

After 'forty years' the cycle begins again. There is no need to count the years or mark off the days when we meet this favourite Old Testament number. 'Forty years' signifies a generation or two, long enough to forget what matters and to relearn it the hard way. This time the Midianites are God's chosen teachers. These nomads with their uncountable camels and their allies from the eastern desert swarm like locusts and devastate Israel's crops as far as Gaza in the farthest west. Israel can only cry to the Lord for help.

An anonymous prophet appears. 'Sent' by the Lord, he begins his message in the proper way: 'Thus says the Lord' (v. 8). In the message reminders of God's goodness far outweigh the reminder of his explicit command and this highlights the starkness of the message's ending. If they have ears to hear, the message is plain: their seven years (another favourite number) of misery is a consequence of their own misdeeds. But there the message ends, with neither announcement of more punishment to come nor good news of imminent rescue.

The story moves on from the prophet with the message to the Israelites to a confusing scene featuring 'the angel of the Lord' with a message for an individual. This is the third angel or 'messenger' (which is what the Hebrew word means) to appear so far (see 2:1ff and 5:23) and another will follow (13:3–23). At first Gideon does not recognize this messenger as any kind of divine visitor at all, though he treats him respectfully (note the 'sir' or 'my lord' in verse 13). In verses 14–19 the writer confuses the messenger and the one who sent him while Gideon continues oblivious to his real identity.

Gideon is the son of no one special from nowhere in particular. He is just a strong and healthy young farmer with enough gumption to harvest a crop against all the odds (verse 11 gives an example) and a healthy scepticism towards religious professionals and their theology. He is not unduly impressed by the way he is addressed (vv. 12–13) nor with the commission he is given (vv. 14–15) and asks for proof of the messenger's credentials (v. 17). He hardly looks like hero material.

2 Three altars and a new name *Read Judges 6:19–40*

Gideon's unmentioned surprise at being told to pour the broth on the ground turns to terror when a touch of the messenger's staff incinerates his extremely generous meal (an ephah of flour is about 10 kilos) and the messenger vanishes. His shock on discovering that he had been talking to a divine messenger leads him, somewhat oddly, to cry to God for help as the Israelites had done in their predicament in verse 6. 'The Lord GOD' in verse 22 is the NRSV's way of showing that the Hebrew here is the divine name plus the title 'Lord'. The altar which he sets up is not mentioned elsewhere. For other stories of setting up and naming altars see Genesis 33:20, 35:7 and Exodus 17:15.

In verse 25 attention moves from the altar called 'The Lord is peace' to the other altar in which Gideon has an interest, the family one to Baal. To add insult to injury the sacred pole (or possibly the wooden image of the goddess Asherah) provides the wood for the sacrifice to the Lord which Gideon offers on the new altar he builds. Contrary to expectations, his father Joash is the first to defend him and to put the fundamental challenge of 'Who is on the Lord's side?' to his fellow Israelites (v. 31). This incident is echoed in the story of Elijah in 1 Kings 18:20–38.

But does Gideon deserve the new name he receives? He may have contended against Baal in pulling down his altar, and he may be a living challenge for Baal to contend against, but he was not brave enough to pull down Baal's altar in daylight. Even after calling out the militia against the gathering Midianites, he twice asks for more proof that God will do what he said he would (vv. 36–40) despite being empowered by God's spirit (v. 34). Compared with Deborah, who went out fearlessly to war without any such empowering by God's spirit, Gideon still cuts a poor figure as a hero.

The tribes of Manasseh, Zebulun and Naphtali had followed Deborah before and they are now joined by Asher (chastened by the taunt in Deborah's song?) (5:17)

3 Preparing for God's battle *Read Judges 7:1–14*

The preparation for battle resumes a theme we have already encountered: Whose battle is it anyway? It is the Lord's! To think otherwise is Israel's perpetual temptation (compare verse 2 with Deuteronomy 8:17). Hence the sifting and weeding out. Quite what happened at the side of the stream is not clear. NRSV rearranges the Hebrew to make it a straight choice between the 300 who lie down and lap the water with their tongues and the 9,700 who kneel down and cup it in their hands. To lie full-length on the ground and lap water with your tongue was not, and is not, a good way to drink out of a stream, which is presumably why so few of them did it. Most translations, however, follow the Hebrew and talk about those who lie full-length on the ground and lap the water with their hands, which doesn't make too much sense. The commentators, ancient and modern, offer all sorts of explanations. However we read it, the point seems to be not simply that the Lord was left with only 300 soldiers, but that he was left with some very strange soldiers indeed, what we might call 300 'oddballs' who were very much lacking in common sense!

Who is giving or taking what in verse 8 is not very clear either, though the 'jars' and 'pitchers' of NRSV and REB are better than the 'provisions' of NIV and NJB.

These 300 not very bright soldiers are led by a leader who is afraid. Verse 10 gives yet another reminder of Gideon's inadequacy, and what follows shows that the Lord both recognizes his fear and offers him a way of overcoming it. Dreams were widely believed to show the future and the one in verse 13 is such a simple and vivid one that the dreamer's comrade has no problem in giving its interpretation. Notice again the David and Goliath proportions, both on the ground between Gideon's 300 and the countless Midianite force (v. 12) and in the dream between a little round barley cake and a tent.

4 The battle *Read Judges 7:15–25*

The story unfolds quickly. 'Thanked God' or 'gave due appreciation to God' is better than 'worshipped' in verse 15. Gideon now knows the certainty of victory and where the credit for it is due and so in rousing the troops he points away from himself to the Lord as well as giving the 300 a place in God's purposes.

The night attack with its crafty ploy is entirely successful, though we are not told who came up with the winning stratagem. Each soldier breaks his jar and blows his ram's horn 'trumpet' (*shofar*). This was a special instrument. In the story of Moses and the giving of the Law on Mount Sinai it is the sound of this instrument which announces the presence of God (Exodus 20:18). It featured in the same special way later on in the temple (as in Psalm 47:5) and it is still used in worship in the great festivals in synagogues today. The story of Joshua and the battle of Jericho in Joshua 6 tells how it was sounded to great effect in the original conquest of Canaan. Its use here is another reminder that this battle is part of God's holy war. The Israelites don't quite get the battlecry right (vv. 18 and 20) but nonetheless it causes the panic by which the Lord destroys the enemy. As so often in Judges the places in verse 22 cannot be identified, but enough is said to show that two different (possibly opposite) directions of flight are intended. The massed enemy is now scattered.

As with Barak and Sisera it is the Lord's victory, and all that is required of the rest of the Israelite militia is to do the mopping up. Men from three of the tribes set off in pursuit of the fleeing enemy (v. 23) and the Ephraimites are called out to block their escape over the Jordan (vv. 24–25). No prisoners are taken (see 8:10). The Ephraimites capture and kill two of the Midianite chiefs, princes or leaders.

5 Mopping up and vengeance *Read Judges 8:1–21*

Gideon's skill with words defuses the situation when the Ephraimites express their feelings of being slighted when there was a chance of action (vv. 1–3).

The Midianites have been routed and Gideon's three hundred are unscathed though exhausted. The towns of Succoth and Penuel, probably Canaanite towns, refuse Gideon's request for provisions on the grounds that the battle isn't over yet and their safety depends on maintaining strict neutrality. Gideon, who is now sure that the Lord will help him, replies with a threat which he subsequently carries out. The threat to Succoth is that he will 'tear' or 'thresh' their flesh 'with' thorns and briars (as with most translations) rather than 'trample' their flesh 'on' them (v. 7) or 'with' them (v. 16) as the NRSV puts it. Here are innocent bystanders caught up in a conflict not of their making. Do they honour Gideon's humanitarian request, backed as it is by ancient codes of hospitality, or do they not? Whatever they do their security is put at risk. Here is one of life's moral complexities for which Gideon has no time at all.

Gideon pursues and captures the two Midianite kings, his

exhausted and still hungry three hundred defeating their remaining fifteen thousand. Panic is again the weapon used, but this time it is wielded by Gideon himself (v. 12). Is this the beginning of the 'by my power' temptation?

In verses 13–17 the threatened vengeance is executed, though no modern translations follow the Hebrew in verse 16 which says that Gideon 'taught them a lesson' with the thorns and briars. The vengeance on Penuel goes way beyond what was threatened. Much inconclusive scholarly debate about levels of literacy in those early times has focused on the young man in verse 14.

Verses 18–21 present difficulties. What happened at Tabor, for no such incident has been mentioned so far? Mount Tabor was the place where Sisera attacked Barak, but that battle was between Israelites and Canaanites, not Midianites, and was several generations ago. What does the kings' first answer mean? Despite uncertainty about these details, the antagonism and arrogance which fuels this exchange is obvious. But what of its wider message? Gideon obviously fails to see the implications of his own words about violence breeding violence.

6 The peace *Read Judges 8:22–35*

Gideon's temptation, hinted at before, materializes in verse 22. He is invited to rule over Israel and promised a dynasty as well. Others, his own son Abimelech first of all, will jump at the chance. Who is king in Israel? is the recurring question in Samuel and Kings. Though Gideon and those like him might insist that the Lord alone is Israel's ruler, the others eventually got their way and, as the Deuteronomic Historian is at pains to point out, paid for it (1 Samuel 8:4–22).

Having insisted that the Lord is king, Gideon sets up a golden 'ephod' to symbolize that fact. This is not the elaborate priestly garment of Exodus 28:5–35 nor the simpler one of 1 Samuel 2:28. Nor is it a box in which sacred stones for casting lots were kept (as in 1 Samuel 14:3). Whatever it is, it is made of 20 kilos of gold, most of which came from the earrings worn by the soldiers (Midianite and Ishmaelite are interchangeable terms for the same people). The clear inference of verse 24 is that Israelite men did no such thing!

Gideon's good intentions lead to the recurring problem of 'images' and their attendant dangers (v. 27). 'Prostitution' is a common metaphor for apostasy (see v. 33 and Exodus 34: 15–16; Hosea 4:12). Nevertheless, while Gideon lives all is well.

With the introduction of Abimelech we meet the theme of good fathers and bad sons which features strongly in the books which follow (e.g. Eli and his two sons, Samuel and his sons, David and Absalom, Solomon and Rehoboam). Abimelech was not an illegitimate son. Though there was a difference in status between marriage (a relationship between two free Israelites) and concubinage (a relationship between a free Israelite man and a slave woman), the children of both relationships were legitimate, as we see from the 'twelve sons of Israel'—four of whom were born to Jacob's concubines.

The saga ends where it began. Memories are short and things relapse. This time 'Baal-berith' (Covenant Lord) is the god of choice. In verse 35 NRSV translates *hesed* as 'loyalty'. This key Old Testament term is traditionally translated as 'steadfast love', and that translation here would bring out more of the pathos of the verse and of the ongoing relationship between God and Israel.

GUIDELINES

Whatever we make of 'angel messengers' in the Old Testament (and they are rather different characters from the angels in heaven of later Christian theology), they are yet another example of the Bible's conviction that God communicates with people. Faith and religion are not only about seeking after truth; because truth is also seeking after us!

I began these readings by saying that one of the issues we would have to face as we read the book of Judges was whether or not such uncongenial stories could be a 'word of the Lord' to us. We have seen that although Judges comes from a world very different from ours, yet there have been some very modern issues touched on in these readings. One has been the question of 'our faith' and 'other faiths'. Another has been the place of nationalisms and ethnicity in our one tiny world. A third has been about the role of women. We might conclude that in this last case the relatively enlightened view of the book can indeed be such a word to us, but we cannot say that about its attitude in the other two cases. Or at least this reader can't. So is there any moral or theological or religious value in the book at all, except perhaps as a warning about what not to do or think?

I think there is. Judges forms part of an explanation about how God's people came to find themselves exiled from his Promised Land. At the same time it was advice about how to stay in the Promised Land when God let them back in again. No doubt many of its attitudes are wrong and its constant theme that goodness is rewarded and wrongdoing is punished is much too rough and ready, but maybe there is enough truth in that theme to make it something of a guideline for living. If in reading Judges we come to grasp that there is such a thing as individual and corporate wrongdoing—no matter how hopelessly old-fashioned and moralistic that word sounds—and that wrongdoing does have consequences, not necessarily for the perpetrators but certainly for others, then perhaps this is its 'word of the Lord' to us after all?

Almighty and everlasting God, you hate nothing that you have made, and forgive the sins of all those who are penitent. Create and make in us new and contrite hearts, that, lamenting our sins and acknowledging our need, we may receive from you, the God of all mercy, perfect forgiveness and peace. Amen.

Further reading

G. Auld, *Joshua, Judges, Ruth*, Daily Study Bible, St Andrew Press

J.D. Martin, *Judges*, Cambridge Bible Commentary, CUP

The Gospel of John (Part 1)

The fourth Gospel is traditionally thought to have been written by the Apostle John in his old age, towards the end of the first century in Ephesus. None of this information is found in the text itself. When apostolic authority was necessary to guarantee the good standing of a gospel or epistle in the Christian church, discussions about authorship could be illuminating. But this is less so nowadays. The fact that this gospel, like the other three, has been received and treasured by the church ought to be enough to afford it a hearing today.

This gospel tells the familiar story found in Matthew, Mark and Luke (the synoptic gospels). But there are significant differences. The sequence of events is altered, with later incidents (the cleansing of the temple and the eucharistic words) brought forward. Jesus moves back and forth between Galilee and Judea. There are healings but no exorcisms, discourses rather than parables. There is a lot about the Holy Spirit, but hardly anything on the kingdom of God, and Jesus says much more about himself, notably in the 'I am' sayings unique to this gospel.

The care with which the gospel has been constructed makes it difficult to see it simply as a supplement to the synoptic gospels. It is better to think of it as an alternative account of Jesus, with an integrity and a 'movement' of its own. The notes, which are based on the Revised Standard Version, try to bring out its movement, as you will see from the headings.

8–14 JUNE — JOHN 1:1—2:12

---

1 From heaven to earth to heaven *Read John 1:1–18*

At the beginning of the Hebrew Bible, the universe owes its genesis to God's creative word: 'Let there be...'. The wisdom literature gives the female figure of Wisdom a role in creation. In

Proverbs 8:22ff she is the first of God's creatures, and takes her place beside him as he goes about his work. Delightful and playful, she links heaven and earth. The apocryphal books of Wisdom and Ecclesiasticus develop these ideas. Here Wisdom shares in God's divinity. She is the power through whom God creates and renews all things: God's glory, light and goodness. She makes people holy, and draws them into God's friendship. She speaks through the prophets (see Wisdom 7:25–27).

Here Wisdom becomes 'Word' (in Greek, *Logos*) in the poetry of God's dealings with the world. The *Logos*—heaven's light and creation's life—comes into the world, and is welcomed by some and rejected by others. A non-biblical poem has Wisdom withdrawing to heaven when she is spurned on earth:

Wisdom could not find a place in which she could dwell;
but a place was found for her in the heavens.
Then Wisdom went out to dwell with the children of the people,
but she found no dwelling place.
So Wisdom returned to her place
and she settled permanently among the angels.

from 1 Enoch 42, translated by John Charlesworth

But not in this Gospel. The light shines so powerfully in the darkness, the heavenly glory is so determined to be seen on earth, that 'the Word became flesh'. Heaven takes the risk of appearing on earth.

Who then is this Word made flesh, this revealer of heavenly light and glory, through whom fellowship with God has been opened up in a new era of grace and truth? Not John the Baptist. He was certainly sent by God, but only as a witness to the true light, the 'only Son of the Father'. The Son may have appeared later than the Baptist. But his flesh has opened the window on heaven's glory and light, and revealed the Father's deep desire for communion with his creatures. In the poetry of God's dealings with the world, 'he who comes after me… was before me'.

Having come from heaven, the Son has now returned to 'the bosom of the Father'. His movement from heaven to earth and back to heaven structures the story we are about to read. What this movement reveals makes the narrative a gospel.

2 From Jerusalem to Bethany *Read John 1:19–28*

The scene shifts dramatically, from the bosom of the Father in heaven to Bethany in the Jordan valley, where the one who came 'to bear witness to the light' is at work. The other gospels indicate John's popularity. Here he is under investigation by Jewish officials sent from Jerusalem.

The priests and Levites were associated with the temple. The Pharisees who sent them were a lay renewal movement, who equated holiness with extending the law of Moses (including the laws which only applied to priests) into every area of life. Their interests were in the synagogues rather than the temple, but at the time of Jesus their influence was growing in Jerusalem. When this gospel was written, the temple had been destroyed and the Pharisees were the torch-bearers of a Jewish future centred no longer on the temple but on the Torah (the law of Moses). This probably accounts for the suggestion in verse 24 that the Pharisees were the leading Jewish group.

The Pharisees' emissaries put John the Baptist on trial. His initial responses are entirely negative. He is not one of the popularly expected figures who would usher in a new age for Israel: neither the Christ (a new David who would defeat Israel's political enemies), nor Elijah (the popular prophet who was expected to return to renew the temple priesthood and its worship; see Malachi 3), nor the prophet like Moses, who would return Israel to the Torah (Deuteronomy 18:18f). Who is he then?

In this gospel he has a very modest role: he is simply a voice. Like the monastic community at Qumran, just across the Jordan valley from where he is baptizing, John applies Isaiah 40:3 to his wilderness work (John may once have been a member of the Qumran community). He sees himself preparing the ground for God to come and liberate Israel from a kind of exile, this time in their own land. His role is modest but highly significant. In his most positive statement so far, he points away from himself to one who is 'coming after me', a man of far greater honour.

John may be on trial here, but even in his modesty he turns the spotlight on his interrogators. They would claim to represent all that Jerusalem stands for: true worship, holiness, devotion to the way of God. But they do not know the one to whom John testifies (v. 26). The physical proximity of the Word made flesh is no guarantee that he will be recognized for who he is. John's trial exposes the spiritual distance between Jerusalem and Bethany—between the emissaries of the Pharisees and those sent by God.

3 From heaven to the Jordan and beyond

Read John 1:29–34

John's testimony to Jesus is aimed at two audiences: the people beside the Jordan, and those who have access to this gospel. In contemporary Jewish writings, 'Lamb of God' and 'Son of God' referred to the messiah. So John's audience at the Jordan would readily have understood his testimony. But this messianic imagery is reinterpreted for the audience of the gospel.

'Lamb of God' anticipates Jesus' passion: in this gospel he dies as the Passover lambs are being slaughtered (the sixth hour on the Day of Preparation for the Passover, according to 19:14). In Exodus 12, the blood of the Passover lamb protected the Israelites from death, so that they would be able to enjoy life in the Promised Land. As the gospel unfolds, we shall see Jesus, the Lamb of God, bringing eternal life to those who have faith in him by overcoming 'the sin of the world', which is unbelief. And this 'life' is nothing less than a share in his own relationship with the Father through the Holy Spirit, which the Son of God gives to those who believe in him.

Notice that there is no report of Jesus' baptism by John here. This is consistent with what we have already seen of the tendency to play down the Baptist's significance in relation to Jesus. There may be more to this than modesty on John's part. It could constitute an appeal by the evangelist to disciples of

John among the audience of the gospel, to allow their master to point *them* to Jesus.

The closest we get to Jesus' baptism is the flashback testimony of verses 32–34, which emphasizes the descent of the Holy Spirit. The evangelist sees this as the most important aspect of the traditions about Jesus' baptism. Notice that the Spirit is twice said to have descended *and remained* on Jesus (vv. 32, 33). The Holy Spirit is an abiding heavenly anointing which Jesus will eventually share with those who *remain* (also translated as 'abide' in chapter 15) in him. So the Baptist points forward to the fruits of Jesus' ministry in making the Holy Spirit available once he has been glorified (7:39; 20:22).

The modest role assigned to John here may tell us as much about the concerns of the evangelist as the Baptist. The portrayal of a prophetic figure who is content to point beyond himself to Jesus is a sharp challenge to any individual or group that gets its own importance out of perspective.

4 From the Baptist to the Messiah *Read John 1:35–42*

However much the evangelist may have been responsible for shaping his material (see yesterday's reading), this is not entirely at the expense of reliable historical information. Verse 30 has the Baptist testify to Jesus: 'After me comes one who ranks before me, for he was before me'. The Greek behind the first four words can also be translated: 'There is a man in my following...'. Several scholars take this to mean that at one time Jesus was a disciple of John.

Today's passage goes on to suggest that Jesus' first disciples were also followers of John. The Baptist's witness bears fruit as some of his own disciples follow Jesus. Notice the sequence: first there is *testimony to Jesus*, which the two disciples *hear*. As a result they *follow* Jesus. Then (in response to Jesus' invitation) they *come and see* where he is staying. Eventually they *stay* (which translates the important Johannine word also rendered by 'remain' or 'abide') with Jesus. They receive no answer to their question 'where are you staying?'. What matters is *that* they stay with Jesus, just as the Spirit stays on him (vv. 32, 33).

Later in the gospel Jesus will promise the Holy Spirit to his disciples, and invite them all to 'stay' in him (chs. 14 and 15).

Next in the sequence of events is the *confession of faith* in Jesus. Seeking leads to finding. Hearing and following result in staying and a deeper kind of seeing. Movement from Bethany to Jesus' lodging place is a metaphor for the development of Johannine faith—from Jesus as 'rabbi' to Jesus as 'messiah'. But the climax of the movement comes when Andrew finds his brother Simon, and voices his own *testimony to Jesus*. The sequence that starts with testimony to Jesus begins again. Simon's change of name symbolizes the deeper changes that take place in him, as he too becomes part of the movement of faith.

The sequence of events in today's reading can be a useful mirror in which we view the development of our own faith. Which parts of the sequence are in place for you or your church, and which parts are missing?

5 From Judea to Galilee *Read John 1:43–51*

Jesus now journeys northwards to Galilee, and calls Philip—a northerner, like Andrew and Simon/Cephas—to become a disciple. As Jesus finds Philip, so Philip finds Nathanael: the disciple imitates his master. Like Andrew in verse 41, Philip testifies to Jesus as the teacher and messiah, referred to by Moses in Deuteronomy 18:18f and the prophets. Nathanael is initially surprised by Philip's testimony to 'Jesus of Nazareth, the son of Joseph', because he judges Jesus by his background—something Jesus' opponents will do later (6:42; 7:41). But Philip is undeterred, and his response to Nathanael echoes Jesus' earlier words to Andrew: 'come and see'. Nathanael is invited to embark on a journey of faith.

Unlike the disciples in yesterday's reading, Nathanael's faith is not so much carried along by *his* knowledge of Jesus as by *Jesus'* knowledge of him. Nathanael's initial judgment of Jesus is an example of seeing him solely in terms of 'flesh', allowing earthly considerations to have the last word. Now Jesus brings heavenly insight to bear on this true Israelite. He sees through his prejudice to an underlying basic integrity.

Further heavenly insight on Jesus' part evokes a confession of faith by Nathanael. 'Son of God' we have heard before. 'King of Israel' is another way of referring to the Davidic messiah. In this gospel it points forward to the passion narrative, where Jesus is interrogated about his kingship by Pontius Pilate (see 18:33ff), and dies as king of the Jews (19:19ff). In his closing remarks Jesus seeks to lead Nathanael beyond a faith based on his power to impress. 'You shall see greater things than these.' What does he have in mind?

Verse 51 alludes to the story of Jacob's dream at Bethel, with the ladder linking earth and heaven and the angels ascending and descending on it (Genesis 28:10ff). Jacob's ladder is now the Son of man, who makes the glory of heaven visible on earth, in his flesh. If Jacob, for all his guile, saw what he did, Nathanael, with all his integrity, will see greater things.

Jesus' promise to Nathanael is hard to fathom. Perhaps there is a clue to what he means in the language of ascending and descending in verse 51. This reminds us of the basic structure of the gospel story: the descent of the heavenly Word made flesh; his ascent to the bosom of the Father; the descent of the Holy Spirit from heaven to remain on Jesus. So what will Nathanael actually see? And when?

6 In Cana on the third day *Read John 2:1–12*

When will Nathanael see the greater things promised by Jesus? Perhaps this 'third day' will reveal all. The attentive reader will recognize the allusion to Easter, when Jesus is glorified. 'On the third day' suggests that the events at Cana are an Easter story, at least in anticipation.

Jesus is apparently invited to the wedding through his mother. Notice that the men he met in Judea by the Jordan have now become 'his disciples'. Their journey north has evidently been more than a geographical shift. They have transferred their allegiance from the Baptist to the Messiah, a movement which John's testimony encouraged.

The wine running out prematurely allows Jesus' promise to

Nathanael to be fulfilled. His initial indifference (the sense of verse 4 is 'what has this concern of yours to do with me?') soon gives way, and behind the scenes activity, directed by his words, results in a surfeit of vintage-quality wine—between 700 and 1000 of today's 75cl bottles! Jesus works in the background: only the servants, and presumably his companions, know the source of the wine, and the bridegroom receives all the credit.

How, then, does this fulfil Jesus' promise to Nathanael, that he will see 'greater things... heaven opened and the angels of God ascending and descending on the Son of man'? The answer lies in the evangelist's insight: this is 'the first of Jesus' signs' and it 'manifested his glory'. In the Bible and later Jewish writings, the splendour of the age of salvation is pictured as a wedding feast with abundant wine (Isaiah 25:6). Or as the day when the dead are raised to life (Daniel 12:1–3). Or as the glory of heaven appearing on earth (Ezekiel 43; Isaiah 60). This 'third day', when abundant wine flows at a wedding banquet, is a sign which points beyond itself to the 'hour (which) has not yet come'—the hour when the Son of man is glorified through the ignominy of execution, when death will surprisingly bear fruit in eternal life (12:23ff).

Nathanael and the others believed in Jesus on the basis of this sign. Easter faith realizes that God does his best work in the background, behind the scenes. And this same faith learns to value surprising and unexpected truths. Something good can indeed come out of Nazareth. And the glory of heaven can be seen in the most unpromising places on earth.

GUIDELINES

Notice the movements in the story so far: from heaven to earth, from Jerusalem to the Jordan, from Judea to Galilee. They involve more than the shift from one place to another. They represent the coming of grace, the desire to know, the growth of faith. Use what you have read to think about the movements in your own life. Where are you aware of the coming of grace, the desire to know, the growth of faith?

Lord, you come into the world
bearing the gifts of grace and truth.
Deepen my desire to know your ways,
and enlarge my vision of your glory.

15–21 JUNE JOHN 2:13—4:26

---

1 To Jerusalem for the Passover *Read John 2:13–22*

From Cana Jesus and his entourage *went down* to Capernaum, before *going up* to Jerusalem for the Passover (the descent–ascent motif again). This gospel uncouples Jesus' action in the temple from his triumphal entry into Jerusalem, and brings it forward to the beginning of his public ministry. On his first visit to Israel's holiest place, Jesus is angry at the trade taking place in the temple courts—the buying and selling of animals for sacrifice, and the purchase of the temple coinage needed for this. Some commentators suggest that Jesus' displeasure was directed towards the temple authorities, who controlled the trade and profited by exploiting the pilgrims, rather than the sacrificial system itself.

When the Jewish leaders ask him for a sign to justify his actions, Jesus offers them a riddle: 'Destroy this temple and in three days I will raise it up'. The Jews take this literally, and refer to the lavish restoration programme started by Herod the Great. This was designed to curry favour with the Jews, and turned the temple into a great job creation scheme. But the evangelist's comment—'he spoke of the temple of his body'—uncovers another layer of meaning.

Devout Jews regarded the temple as the focus of God's glory and his dwelling place on earth. Its architecture, dividing Jews from Gentiles, men from women, priests from the people, expressed an understanding of holiness as separation from all that was considered unclean. In this holy place, the glory and purity of heaven were represented on earth.

'Zeal for thy house will consume me': Psalm 69:9 suggests

that Jesus' devotion to God is such that his own body will be destroyed. 'Destroy this temple, and in three days I will raise it up.' 'For *temple*, read *body*,' urges the evangelist: Jesus is making a cryptic reference to his crucifixion. 'For *body* read *temple*': Jesus' crucified and risen body—the summit of his self-sacrificing devotion—is *the* place where heaven and earth meet, and God's glory and holiness are at their most intense (cf 1:51).

The penny dropped for the disciples after Easter. Only then did the psalm text make sense of Jesus' riddle. Beyond the third day—which is the era of faith in Jesus Christ in the church—we too can begin to appreciate the radical reinterpretation of the nature of God held out here. 'He came to his own home, and his own people received him not' (1:11). Far from banishing God's glory to the heavens, what happened to his body in Jerusalem at Passover gave it a new location. The evangelist could write on behalf of all believers: 'We have beheld his glory' (1:14).

2 To Jesus by night *Read John 2:23—3:12*

Jesus' encounter with Nathanael showed something of his heavenly insight (1:47ff). His meeting with Nicodemus reveals more. Because Jesus 'knew what was in a man', he did not trust himself to those whose faith depended on miracles. Faith like this is inadequate—and it is found in 'a man of the Pharisees', Nicodemus, a high-ranking teacher of the Law and a member of the Jewish ruling council. Nicodemus appears several times in the gospel, but as we shall see, he remains a man of inadequate faith.

Nicodemus speaks for others: 'Rabbi, *we* know that you are a teacher come from God'. Jesus' words in verse 7 are addressed to them: '*you* (plural) must be born again'. In verse 11, Jesus also speaks for others: '*we* speak of what we know... but *you* (plural) do not receive *our* testimony'. So Jesus' conversation with Nicodemus can also be read as a dialogue between two groups.

The notes on 1:29–34 referred to the way this gospel addresses two audiences: one around Jesus, and another which has access to the gospel. David Rensberger suggests that Nicodemus represents a Jewish group in the evangelist's world who respect Jesus as a 'teacher come from God', but no more. To go further would mean breaking their links with the synagogue. Relations are not good between the evangelist's church and the synagogue, which has no place for those who confess Jesus as Messiah (see 9:22).

Nicodemus' people must be 'born anew' (in Greek *anothen*) in order to enter the kingdom of God. What does this entail? The Greek is ambiguous: it can mean 'anew' in the sense of 'again', or 'from above'. Nicodemus thinks Jesus is referring to a literal birth, but his misunderstanding draws out Jesus' real meaning. 'Born *anothen*' means 'born of water and the Spirit' (v. 5) and 'born of the Spirit' (v. 6). 'Born of water' refers to Christian baptism, 'born of the Spirit' to full Johannine faith in Jesus (in 1:12–13 those who are 'born of God' believe in Jesus and become children of God). Jesus rejects the traditional belief that being born as a Jew is sufficient for God's kingdom (v. 6). If his alternative baffles Nicodemus, then he should realize that it is no more mysterious than the operation of the wind.

So the evangelist uses Jesus' conversation with Nicodemus to appeal to a group in his own world whose faith is inadequate. In their respect for Jesus, they have made a start, but they need to go further by being 'born from above'. If they are serious about the kingdom of God, they should make the full Christian profession of faith in Jesus, be baptized and join the evangelist's community, even if this means leaving the synagogue. This will demand great courage on their part, but it will bring them out of the darkness of night (v. 2) into the daylight of God's glory.

3 Light and life from heaven *Read John 3:13–21*

Nicodemus' bold assertion about what he and his group know (v. 2) begins to look rather bare by verse 10. How much do they *really* know about God, the Spirit, the kingdom? So far Jesus has been using 'earthly' images—birth, wind—to convey his message, and Nicodemus has found these difficult. How then can this 'teacher of Israel' grasp the full 'heavenly' meaning behind his statement that Jesus is a 'teacher come from God'?

In verses 13–21 Jesus presents his heavenly testimony to Nicodemus and his people. His words gather up the full Johannine faith in the one sent from heaven to earth, Jesus the 'Word become flesh' who has now returned to 'the bosom of the Father'. As the Son of Man, he brings heaven and earth together, and so is well qualified to reveal the mysteries of God (v. 13; cf. 1:51). The 'lifting up' of the Son of Man in verse 14 has a double meaning: hoisting him on to the cross, and elevating him to heaven. Jesus' true honour lies in his shame. God's glory is found in the temple of his body.

Like Moses' serpent in Numbers 21:4–9, Jesus' lifting up brings life. Verse 16 goes further by presenting his passion as the revelation of God's love. Just as Abraham was prepared to sacrifice his only son Isaac (Genesis 22), so God gives up his 'only Son' Jesus. As in 1:10, the 'world' here is humanity in all its hostility towards its creator, and is represented by, but certainly not restricted to, the leaders of the Jews. In Jewish belief, eternal life is always accompanied by judgment. Both are now revealed in the coming of Jesus, and faith in him as 'the only Son of God' in the full Johannine sense is the criterion for salvation.

The dualism in verses 19–21 may suggest that people have no real choice about salvation or judgment: their responses to the light are already fixed by whether or not their actions are 'evil' or 'true'. But the steady appeal throughout the gospel for a change of heart and growth in faith, 'so that the world might be saved through him' (v. 17), counts against rigid determinism. Dualism can be a useful way of tidying up a messy world. Its sharp contrast between light and darkness may be appropriate when the alternative courses of action are so clear and contrasting, as Jesus and the evangelist evidently believed about their respective worlds. But we will often find ourselves wondering what this dualistic language means in our grey areas, where light and dark shade into one another.

4 Testimony from above *Read John 3:22–36*

The connections between this and the rest of chapter 3 may not be immediately obvious, but there is a link. In verses 1–21, Jesus appealed to Nicodemus and his people to make the full Johannine confession of faith. In this passage, John the Baptist calls on his own followers to do the same.

There are historical details here not found in the other gospels. Jesus also had a ministry of baptism, not far from John. There was a certain amount of rivalry between them, at least in the public's perception. The persistence of this rivalry into the evangelist's world would explain his desire to highlight the importance of Jesus at the expense of John.

Earlier in the gospel, John testified to Jesus before Jews sent from Jerusalem (see 1:19ff). Now he testifies before his own disciples. His modesty comes across in the wedding imagery: he is simply the 'friend of the bridegroom' who is full of joy because the one whose coming he announced has finally arrived. This is John's last appearance in the gospel, whose unfolding story will only bear out the truth of his words: 'he must increase, but I must decrease' (v. 30).

Verses 31–36 pick up a number of themes from Jesus' conversation with Nicodemus. Like verse 13, verse 31 refers to Jesus' heavenly origins ('from above', *anothen*, is found in vv. 3 and 7), and the contrast between heaven and earth echoes verse 12. Reference to Jesus' testimony in verse 11 is repeated in verse 32, and amplified in verses 33–35. Mention of the Spirit in verse 34 takes us back to verse 8. The contrast in verse 36 between faith in the Son leading to eternal life and unbelief bringing about condemnation is also found in verses 16–18.

These repetitions allow John the Baptist to address his disciples in the same way that Jesus spoke to Nicodemus and his people. David Rensberger suggests that the evangelist uses the Baptist's testimony to appeal to another group in his own world whose faith is inadequate—those who still hold John the Baptist in high regard. If they are truly John's disciples, they will allow their master to point them to Jesus. They too need to be born 'from above' and make the full Christian confession of faith.

The evangelist's world, like that of Jesus, was marked by debates within the Jewish family over identity, the result of pressure from powerful Gentile forces. In today's world, rival religious groups are encouraged to learn how to respect and tolerate one another, not least because of the potential for violence on a grand scale. The worlds may be different, but the demand for truth and justice is the same. How might this evangelist's story of Jesus help us today?

5 In Samaria at midday *Read John 4:1–15*

The evangelist's interest in groups on the edges of his own community continues, as he turns his attention to Samaritans. The inhabitants of Samaria lived in the area between Judea and Galilee. They were descended from Jews, left behind after the deportation in 722BC when Samaria fell to the Assyrians, and foreigners whom the Assyrians resettled there. We hardly need reminding that there was no love lost between Jews and Samaritans.

Verses 1 and 2—a rather clumsy opening—give the impression that Jesus' baptism movement in Judea was growing in strength, and drawing hostility from Pharisees there. Verse 2 contradicts 3:22, and looks like a later editorial addition, designed to play down the similarities between Jesus and John the Baptist.

The inhabitants of Sychar would have valued their well not simply as a source of water, but also as a link with the patriarch Jacob. This would have allowed them to counter Jewish disdain by claiming some honour for their community. A public conversation between a Jewish male and a Samaritan woman would have been considered doubly improper (see vv. 9 and 27). What could possibly be the motives of such a man and woman?

Their conversation is ostensibly about water. The woman takes Jesus literally, just as Nicodemus did when he spoke about birth. But once again her misunderstanding draws out Jesus' true meaning (by now this has become a familiar Johannine technique). Jesus is speaking metaphorically: 'living water' is not simply water from a spring or well. What is he referring to?

We should not lose sight of the baptismal context provided by the previous chapter, whose 'water' theme extends into chapter 4. The woman could not possibly know 'the gift of God and who it is that is saying to you, "Give me a drink"' (v. 10). But the readers know. As John the Baptist testified, the gift of God is the Holy Spirit, which has descended from heaven to remain on Jesus. And Jesus is the one who baptizes with the Holy Spirit (1:32–33). Jesus, then, does not have access to an inexhaustible supply of spring water, as the woman initially thinks. His 'living water' can only be the Holy Spirit: in due course, thirsty believers will experience 'rivers of living water' flowing 'out of the heart' (7:38f).

There are parallels between Jesus' conversation with the Samaritan woman and his earlier words with Nicodemus. The metaphor may be different, but the intention is the same: to encourage another marginal group into the fulness of Christian faith and life. At this stage, we cannot say how the woman will respond, but the outcome looks promising. Nicodemus came to Jesus by night; she has her conversation in the bright light of midday.

6 On this mountain? *Read John 4:16–26*

At first sight Jesus' mention of the woman's husband looks like a red herring, though the marriage theme has been around in the narrative since Cana. Jesus is giving her the chance to find out more about him (cf v. 10). His heavenly insight allows him to see into the heart of a woman as well as a man (cf 1:48, 2:25). She realizes that someone as perceptive as this can only be a prophet, and so she questions him about an issue that divides Jews and Samaritans—the legitimacy of their temple on Mount Gerizim. In order to validate its claims, the Samaritans identified the mount with several holy sites mentioned in the Pentateuch, including Bethel, where Jacob had his dream (Genesis 28).

For the evangelist, the woman raises the deeper issue of the identity of the true faith community, where God is worshipped and his will is revealed. Is this associated with particular places venerated by racial or religious groups, who are often antagonistic towards one another? Jesus' remarks in verse 22 are those of a loyal Jew, but he refers to an 'hour' when tribal loyalties will count for nothing.

Jesus contrasts 'worship on this mountain... (and) in Jerusalem' with 'worship... in spirit and truth'. He is not differentiating between the material and the spiritual in worship—outward versus inward, ritual versus faith—but pointing to a communion with God which transcends the accidents of natural birth. Those who 'worship the Father in spirit and truth' are born from God, from above, of water and the Spirit. Living water wells up in them to eternal life. They belong to the community which believes that 'grace and truth came through Jesus Christ' (1:17). Their temple is Jesus' crucified and exalted body (2:21).

'Worship in spirit and truth' makes eternal life accessible to marginalized groups like the Samaritans. Their representative, the woman, now reveals her growing spiritual insight, as she begins to make the connection between Jesus' words and her people's expectations. The Samaritans' messiah would be the prophet like Moses (Deuteronomy 18:18), and he was expected to restore their temple and its worship. Is Jesus addressing the hopes of Samaritans, and at the same time setting them on a broader canvas?

It would appear so. He declares his true identity, for the first time in this gospel: 'I who speak to you am he,' or in the Greek: '*Ego eimi* ("I am", the divine name), who speaks to you'. The intention of all worship—communion with God in community—is realized in him.

GUIDELINES

The movement of grace from heaven to earth is matched by the movement from the centre to the margins. Jesus journeys from Jerusalem to Galilee and Samaria. The evangelist appeals to members of the synagogue and the followers of the Baptist. Heaven and earth, Jerusalem and the regions are linked by the movement of love. The same is true of the community of Christian believers and the wider world.

The church can never allow the way the story of Jesus is received—by groups on the margins of its life, and beyond—to determine its response to an indifferent and sometimes hostile world. Mission is always a movement of love.

Lord, as I read this gospel,
remind me of the movement of your grace.
And as I behold your glory,
draw me into the mission of your love.

22–28 JUNE JOHN 4:27—5:47

---

1 Into the Samaritan city *Read John 4:27–42*

The return of Jesus' disciples sends the woman back to her own people. But she does not leave the scene to avoid public shame: she abandons her water jar to become a missionary. Back in her city, she invites people to 'come (and) see'—a typical Johannine summons to begin a journey of faith (cf 1:39, 46).

Meanwhile the disciples and Jesus discuss food, as he and the woman had earlier talked about water. Like her, the disciples take him literally at first, which gives him the chance to talk about the deeper meaning of 'my food'. If 'living water' is a metaphor of the Holy Spirit, then 'food' symbolizes Jesus' submission to his Father's will and his desire to do his work. What does this entail?

Jesus uses agricultural metaphors to spell out what he means by his 'food'. But he gives a twist to the popular proverbs in verses 35 and 37. In the natural order, sowing and reaping are separated by 'four months'. But his heavenly work is not subject to any earthly interval. His conversation with the Samaritan woman has sown seeds of faith which will be harvested during the two days he 'stays' with them (cf 1:39).

Once again the narrative shows the development of a person's faith. The woman begins by seeing Jesus as a Jewish man; he becomes a prophet, then *the* prophet, the Messiah and finally 'the Saviour of the world'. But there is more to the story than this. An unnamed Samaritan woman succeeds where Nicodemus the teacher of Israel fails: she comes to believe in Jesus as Messiah, and expresses her faith openly. What's more, her testimony brings others to faith. In this sense she is a true missionary, like Mary Magdalene at Easter, the first to testify to the resurrection of Jesus (20:18).

We must not forget that she remains a Samaritan. If there were Samaritans in, or on the edges of, the evangelist's church, this story would speak powerfully to them. Like the Jews, the Samaritans' hopes of a Messiah are fulfilled by Jesus. Their longing for communion with God 'in spirit and truth' is met in him. In the Johannine community, entered by baptism and faith in Jesus Christ, the living water of the Spirit wells up to eternal life for Samaritans too. Among those who believe in the Saviour of *the world*, there is no room for the prejudice which despises race or gender.

2 Back to Cana in Galilee *Read John 4:43–54*

Jesus returns to Cana after travelling though the main regions of Palestine. Verse 44 suggests that Jerusalem is his 'own country'. There, as we shall see increasingly, 'he came to his own home, and his own people received him not' (1:11).

In verse 46 the evangelist alerts us to what happened last time Jesus was in Cana. Now the problem is much more serious than a lack of wine. The son of a high-ranking official—a servant of the governor, Herod Antipas—is gravely ill. Like Jesus' mother at the wedding feast, the father begs him to help. Jesus' immediate response in verse 48 reminds us of the seeming rebuke to his mother in 2:4. Here, though, Jesus does not so much censure the official (which would have been heartless) as issue a wider challenge. 'You' is plural—'unless you people see signs and wonders...'. Neither in Jerusalem nor in Galilee will Jesus trust himself to those whose faith relies on his power to produce signs.

The official does not come into this category. His response to Jesus' words in verse 50 shows that he has the kind of faith Jesus approves of. He is prepared to take Jesus at his word: he obeys him, and trusts that what he says is true. The evangelist highlights the way this faith is rewarded. The official's son is healed at the very moment when Jesus says, 'Your son will live'. True faith relies on the word of Jesus, with its power to bring life in the face of death.

Is there any place, then, for 'signs and wonders' in faith? The gospel so far has given out mixed messages. At the wedding in Cana, the disciples believed in Jesus on the basis of the sign, but in Jerusalem Jesus was wary of such faith. For Nicodemus and his people, Jesus' signs lent weight to his authority as a 'teacher come from God', but Jesus found their faith inadequate. The Galilean official clearly believes that Jesus has the power to heal, and his faith meets with approval. What are we to make of this?

As the gospel story progresses we shall see that there is a place for 'signs and wonders', but as 'signs' and not ends in themselves. They point beyond themselves, by revealing something of the character of the one who performs them. Religion always finds room for remarkable people and spectacular actions, with their undoubted power to impress. But it is easy to be so taken up with the spectacle as to lose sight of the object of faith. Where is this true today?

3 Up to Jerusalem *Read John 5:1–9*

The evangelist has used the first four chapters of the gospel to testify to Jesus' identity and mission. The second sign at Cana forms an important bridge to the next section of the gospel, chapters 5–12. In yesterday's reading Jesus was asked to 'come down' to Capernaum to heal a dying boy. What in fact 'came down' was his life-giving word: 'Go, your son will live'. Now Jesus 'goes up' to Jerusalem for an unnamed feast. The descent–ascent motif here reminds us that this movement of the Word brings life to the world. From here in the gospel, we shall see how Jesus' encounters with Jerusalem contribute to his lifting up from the world and return to the Father.

Though the feast is unspecified, verse 2 is full of detail. The pool is not far from the temple area, and the people surrounding it live on the margins of Jewish society. They are reduced to begging, and according to verse 4 (omitted from some manuscripts) depend on superstition for their wellbeing. They are as good as dead. Jesus singles out one of them. At first sight his question seems absurd: of course the man wants to be healed! But Jesus is interested in his psychological as well as his physical state. Long-term dependency is not easily overcome. When illness is internalized, it becomes even more crippling than its physical manifestation. Verse 7 is an implicit 'yes' to Jesus' question. Again we see the power of Jesus' life-giving word in the face of death: 'at once the man was healed'—physically and psychologically, and as he found his way into mainstream society once more, socially and spiritually too.

Verse 9 ends ominously: 'now that day was the Sabbath'. We know from the synoptic gospels that Jesus clashed with some Pharisees over his attitude to the Sabbath day. Under pressure from Gentile culture and an empire whose authority now extended into the heart of their ancestral land, the Jewish people had come to regard Sabbath observance as a vital way of maintaining their identity and solidarity. Opinions varied as to what was allowed on the Sabbath. Jesus would not have been out of line with some Jewish groups, but as we shall see, the more zealous among them were affronted by what they saw as his total disregard for the word of God. In his desire to bring life, Jesus is about to find himself on the threshold of death.

4 On the Sabbath, in the temple *Read John 5:9b–18*

The location of the man's healing is significant. It takes place in the shadow of the temple, the symbolic centre of a religion which separated sacred and profane. By contravening the Sabbath, Jesus blurs the distinction between holiness and godlessness. But the now revitalized man initially bears the brunt of the authorities' censure. It is difficult to know what he should have done with his mattress, which was perhaps his only possession. Was he to leave it by the pool, and lose it as a result?

Meanwhile Jesus moves out of the limelight, to avoid unwelcome attention from those likely to be impressed by signs and wonders. He eventually finds the man in the temple, where he has doubtless come to give thanks to God. Now he can also take part in the Jewish festivals—another dimension of his healing. Jesus' remarks in verse 14 are puzzling. Is he suggesting that the man's paralysis was the result of sin? Does he concur with those who think he was behaving unlawfully by carrying his mattress? Or is he addressing what the man himself believed about the cause of his misfortune and the condition for his future wellbeing? If he is doing the last of these, then Jesus makes no attempt to overturn in an instant what generations had believed and taught about suffering. As we shall see, the gospel as a whole certainly severs the connection between sin and suffering.

The Jewish authorities eventually catch up with Jesus. They do not merely question, they 'persecute' him. This strong language marks the start of Jesus' trial. Historically, this gospel sheds light on the relationship between Jesus and the Jewish authorities by suggesting that the debates between them occurred over a much longer period than the last week of Jesus' life. Theologically, the point at issue is Jesus' status and authority. He justifies his Sabbath activity, not by pointing to the priority of meeting human need (as in Mark 2:27: 'the Sabbath was made for people, not people for the Sabbath'), but by claiming to do the work of God.

'My Father is working still and I am working.' It is not that Jesus claims to be God. Then he would be a threat only to his own sanity, and hardly worthy of the sustained interest of the authorities. As we shall see, identifying his works and teaching with God proves to be far more subversive. It calls into question the temple's work and teaching, and all they represent, and threatens to unseat its privileged élites. It also carries a radically different understanding of God. His holiness and glory are no longer associated with the splendid architecture of temples but the godless form of a man lifted up from the earth.

5 Before the Jewish authorities *Read John 5:19–30*

Jesus begins his defence by explaining his statement in verse 17. This is the first of several discourses which follow and interpret Jesus' signs.

Verse 19 states the basis on which Jesus claims to be doing God's work. Try reading it first without the capital letters, as a domestic proverb about the relationship between fathers and sons: 'a son can do nothing of his own accord, but only what he sees his father doing'. The proverb has been transformed into a theological statement about the relationship between Jesus and his heavenly Father. Notice that their relationship is one of love: because the Father loves the Son, he initiates him into all his ways. So the authorities can expect 'greater things' than they have seen in the revitalizing of the paralysed man.

In verses 21–29, Jesus speaks about two kinds of work delegated to him by his Father: raising the dead to life in the age to come, and exercising judgment on the last day. Jews thought of these as particular works of God, alongside his sustaining the world. Notice that in verse 21, the Son already 'gives life to whom he will', as evidenced by the second sign in Cana and the Sabbath healing in Jerusalem. And as the Son of man who has come down from heaven (the Son of man is the agent of the last judgment in many Jewish writings; cf Matthew 25:31ff), Jesus already exercises God's judgment, in the sense that response to him determines whether one is saved or condemned (vv. 23–24; cf. 3:18ff).

The Johannine emphasis on the 'already' of Jesus' divine work does not rule out what he will do in the future: hence the reference to the coming 'hour' in verses 25 and 28. But this gospel is more concerned with what he does in the present: 'the hour is coming, *and now is*...' (v. 25). Those who know the whole story will recognize the allusion to the raising of Lazarus here (see chapter 11). There will be no shortage of evidence to support Jesus' claim that he is acting on God's authority and doing his Father's will.

6 Testimony from earth or heaven? *Read John 5:31–47*

A Jewish court of law required the testimony of two witnesses. Here Jesus calls on *four* to corroborate his claim to be acting on behalf of God. First there is John the Baptist. 'You sent to John'—so his opponents can hardly be ignorant of his testimony. 'He was not the light' (1:8), but as 'a burning and shining lamp' he lit the way to Jesus as the Lamb of God and Son of God.

Secondly there are Jesus' works, delegated to him by the Father. Notice that they are referred to here as 'works' rather than 'signs' to emphasize their divine authority. What Jesus does is of a piece with God's archetypal work of raising the dead and judging the world. The third witness is the Father himself, who has testified to Jesus by giving the Holy Spirit to him as an abiding presence (1:32ff). The Father's testimony is mediated through John the Baptist (1:33), which heightens the importance of his witness to Jesus. Unfortunately the divine testimony is wasted on these Jewish leaders. Jesus is severe in his condemnation: 'his voice you have never heard, his form you have never seen, and you do not have his word abiding in you'. Their knowledge of God is judged by their response to Jesus. As the Son of man from heaven, he has heard God's voice and seen his form; and as the Word made flesh, he has God's word abiding in him.

The fourth witness follows naturally from the third. As Israel's teachers, the Jewish leaders quarried the scriptures in order to apply them to every detail of life. But for all their zeal, they missed the essential scriptural message. Many people in Jesus' day believed that the scriptures would find their true meaning in the age of salvation, the time of the Messiah. On this understanding, Jesus can claim Moses as a witness to himself.

Four witnesses—yet 'you refuse to come to me that you may have life'. Why is this? Jesus seems to suggest that it all comes down to the state of the heart. These Jewish leaders do not really love God and believe Moses. Instead they are seduced by their status in the system which makes so much of the accidents of birth, the place of the temple and Sabbath observance.

Jesus concludes his defence by laying bare what really matters to them. In the end, their trust in the honour given to them by other people rather than God will be their undoing.

GUIDELINES

Jewish people at the time of Jesus looked forward to the coming of a new world in which present injustices would be removed, and God's creation would finally come into its own. Those who entered this world would have 'eternal life', which literally means 'life in the (coming) age'. We have read that eternal life 'is coming, and now is', in the work of Jesus. But it is not always recognized as such.

Those who believe in Jesus can see the world coming to life through the movement of grace, the mission of love. But there is no story to be told of assured success, only a gospel of courageous devotion to the Father's will.

Save me, Lord, from the delusion of thinking
that living in the way of love will always bring
success or happiness.
Let your word of life be sufficient
to revitalize faith and rekindle hope.

29 JUNE–5 JULY — JOHN 6:1–71

1 In Galilee once more: across the sea to the mountain

Read John 6:1–15

Jesus concluded his defence before the Jerusalem authorities by appealing to Moses: 'he wrote of me'. The material in this chapter shows what he meant. There are some obvious connections between today's reading and the story of Moses. Like him, Jesus goes up the mountain. Verse 4 mentions Passover. The hungry crowds remind us of the Israelites in the wilderness. Jesus' question in verse 5 echoes Moses' prayer in Numbers 11:13, 'where am I to get meat to give to all this people?' Jesus' acclaim as 'the prophet who is to come into the world' matches Moses' expectation in Deuteronomy 18:18. Later on, the crowds murmur at Jesus as the Israelites complained to Moses. So we are invited to set this story of Jesus alongside that of Moses, and interpret one in the light of the other.

The centrepiece of this feeding story is the conversation between Jesus and the two disciples Philip and Andrew. Unlike the other gospels, Jesus takes the initiative in meeting the crowd's needs. With his heavenly insight, he knows what he will do. Philip realizes that human resources are utterly inadequate: 'We couldn't possibly buy enough bread; we'd need more than six months' wages!' The only food available is a few barley loaves (the food eaten by the poor) and a couple of dried fish. But these prove sufficient for Jesus to feed the crowd, with enough leftovers to fill twelve baskets.

The crowds know what to make of the feeding. They spot the connection with Moses: the messiah-king was expected to repeat the manna miracle. But what of today's readers? Those who are comfortable with divine intervention find no problems. 'God can suspend the so-called laws of nature as and when he wishes, and if Jesus is equal with God, what is to prevent a miracle like this?' Those less at ease with this approach may be drawn to a more rational explanation. 'The boy's generosity encouraged others to share what food they had, so that everyone was satisfied.' Both these interpretations miss the point. Whatever actually happened, all the gospels see the feeding as symbolic, and none more than this one.

The emphasis here is on the initiative and action of Jesus. 'My Father is working still, and I am working' (5:17): the feeding is another instance of Jesus doing his Father's work. 'Moses wrote of me' (5:46). Just as God fed the Israelites in the wilderness, so Jesus feeds the crowds at Passover-tide. We must wait for the true significance of this feeding until we reach the other side of the sea (vv. 25ff).

2 Back across the sea *Read John 6:16–21*

The sequence of events after the feeding is different here from the other gospels, but Matthew, Mark and John all include the story of the disciples' hazardous journey back across the lake, and Jesus' coming to them across the water. The Sea of Galilee is notorious for its sudden storms. In view of the way the evangelist has underlined the connections with Moses, Jesus' mysterious walking on the water is reminiscent of the Israelites' crossing the Red Sea.

Some of the psalms shed light on this story. For example, Psalm 77:19–20 has God walking 'through the sea': the Hebrew can also be translated as '*on* the sea'. Psalm 78:13 and 24 mention the crossing of the Red Sea and the manna in the wilderness. Psalm 107:23ff includes a number of striking parallels:

Some went down to the sea in ships...
they saw the deeds of the Lord,
his wondrous works in the deep.
For he commanded, and raised the stormy wind,
which lifted up the waves of the sea. ...
Their courage melted away in their evil plight...
(they) were at their wits' end.
Then they cried to the Lord in their trouble,
and he delivered them in their distress...
he brought them to their desired haven.

'My Father is working still, and I am working' (5:17). By feeding the crowds and walking on the water, Jesus is doing the work of God. The brevity of the narrative brings Jesus' words to the fore: 'It is I (*Ego eimi*); do not be afraid'. The one who spoke to Moses at the burning bush as *Ego eimi* (in the Greek version of Exodus 3:14) now reveals himself in Jesus, the Word made flesh, the Son who does his Father's work.

We can see, then, how the evangelist uses these unusual stories of feeding and walking on water. They are signs which point beyond themselves to the mystery of Jesus. He is rightly perceived as teacher and liberator: the prophet like Moses, the messiah-king. But there is more to him: in the words of the late

John Robinson, Jesus is *a window into God at work... the human face of God*. As we arrive with the boat at the shore, we can expect to discover more of what this mystery holds.

3 In the synagogue at Capernaum *Read John 6:22–34*

Once the storm has died down, the crowds make the same journey as the disciples, back across the lake to Capernaum. Note their search for the increasingly elusive Jesus: only in verse 59 are we told that they find him in the synagogue. This is a place of communion with God in worship and prayer, and with others in fellowship. Jesus is found where God and people meet.

Jesus is wary of these Galileans, as he was of the Judeans at another Passover in Jerusalem. Earlier they had tried to force him to lead them in a revolt against Rome (v. 15). 'You seek me... because you ate your fill of the loaves'—hardly surprising, in view of the poverty to which imperial taxation had reduced Galilean peasants at that time. But Jesus wants them to consider another kind of food. His words about eternal life pick up the thread that runs through his conversations with Nicodemus, the Samaritan woman, the official at Cana and the authorities in Jerusalem.

The audience ask the one who does God's work how *they* can 'labour' for the food he offers. We might expect Jesus to refer to Moses, as he does when others ask about eternal life (see Mark 10:17ff). But instead he asks for faith. Faith in his Father is the food that sustains him in his mission (4:34). Now he asks his audience to have the same faith in him as God's emissary. But does Jesus have any way of authorizing his leadership, as Moses did by providing manna in the wilderness?

Jesus replies with a discourse in the style of a synagogue sermon, structured around texts from the Law and the Prophets. He begins with Exodus 16:15 (supplied by the audience): 'He gave them bread from heaven to eat' (v. 31). Later on, he refers to Isaiah 54:13: 'they shall all be taught by God' (v. 45). At the end he returns to the Exodus text (vv. 48–51). So the narrative moves from scriptural allusions in the stories of the feeding and the walking on the sea, to direct quotation and explanation, to demonstrate how it is that 'Moses wrote of me'.

Who gave them 'bread from heaven to eat'? Not Moses, says Jesus, but 'my Father'. And what of this bread? The true bread is not perishable manna, which must be gathered every day and used up quickly. 'The bread of God… comes down from heaven and gives life to the world.' Jesus can only be referring to himself. He now begins to reveal what his feeding of the five thousand symbolizes.

4 Bread from heaven *Read John 6:35–51*

If verse 34 is a typical Johannine misunderstanding, it invites Jesus to explain what he means by 'bread from heaven'. 'I am the bread of life' is the first of the distinctive 'I am' sayings which are only found in this gospel. Behind them lies the use of 'I am' as a divine name in late Judaism. Jesus draws on a series of images—bread; light; door; good shepherd; resurrection and life; way, truth and life; vine—to express the way in which he does God's work.

'Bread of life' reminds us of scriptural references to God's word and wisdom. In Isaiah 55, the thirsty and hungry are summoned to 'come', 'drink' and 'eat'—metaphors for seeking and listening to God, living in his ways, finding joy and blessing. In Proverbs 9:5f, Wisdom issues the invitation to 'come, eat of my bread and drink of the wine I have mixed'—metaphors again for living 'in the way of insight'. Verse 35 echoes the apocryphal work Ecclesiasticus 24:21, where Wisdom announces: 'Those who eat of me will hunger for more; those who drink of me will thirst for more.' As the bread of life, Jesus' obedience to the Father and his life-giving power provide the nourishment to sustain believers in this world and in the age to come.

For the first time in this gospel, Jesus' teaching brings about a division between believers and unbelievers in the same audience. Those who 'murmur' are like the Israelites who complain in the wilderness (see Exodus 16). They can only see Jesus in terms of the accidents of birth and family. In this sense their complaints remind us of the first words of Nathanael in the gospel: 'can anything good come out of Nazareth?' (1:46). But unlike him, these grumblers are unwilling to set out on the journey of faith—to be drawn by the Father and 'taught by God', as the prophet required (v. 45). Because he has seen the Father and come from God, Jesus is well qualified to teach God's word and issue Wisdom's invitation.

Jesus provokes a crisis in his synagogue audience. Are they content with death, or do they want eternal life? Moses' manna did not overcome death, but Jesus claims that his bread does. There is more, though, to 'the bread of life' than heavenly teaching, however wise. 'The bread which I shall give for the life of the world is my flesh.' Division and hostility will bring rejection and eventually death to Jesus. But it is precisely this death—the giving of his flesh in obedience to his Father—that will nourish those who believe with eternal life.

Bread from heaven is crucified flesh. Like the temple as Jesus' body (2:21), and his execution as exaltation and love (3:14ff), this is yet another invitation to 'see' differently, and to work out what it means to live accordingly.

5 Bread from heaven to eat *Read John 6:52–59*

So far Jesus has been explaining the meaning of 'he gave them bread from heaven'. The Jews' question in verse 52 invites him to explain what it means to 'eat' this heavenly bread given by God. Eating might simply mean faith in Jesus: those who 'come' to him as the bread of life and 'eat' (v. 35) are people who 'see the Son and believe in him' (v. 40). But verse 53 introduces the new idea of drinking Jesus' blood. If 'eating' simply means 'believing', what is the point of this additional image? There are good reasons for thinking that 'eating' and 'drinking' refer to the eucharist. Verse 56 reminds us of chapter 15, with its talk of 'abiding' in Jesus as the 'true vine'. This image has eucharistic overtones, and chapters 13–17 are set at the last supper. It is unlikely that Christians in the evangelist's audience would hear about eating and drinking Jesus' flesh and blood without being reminded of the eucharist.

In this gospel, unlike the others, there is no mention of Jesus' institution of the Lord's Supper. What if the evangelist has brought his 'last supper' material forward, just as he did with Jesus' action in the temple in 2:13ff? This would allow him to highlight the connection between Jesus' continuing confrontation with 'the Jews' and his passion, and to remind believers that 'the shamefully crucified Jesus is the life-giving Son of God' (Rensberger). His gift of eternal life is mediated though the church's eucharistic worship. Here believers are nourished by the bread and wine which symbolize Jesus' devotion to his Father's will in the ultimate act of self-giving love for the world.

The likelihood of a sacramental interpretation is strengthened by links with Jesus' earlier conversation with Nicodemus. His question in 3:4—'how can a person be born again...?'—is similar to the Jews' question in verse 52: 'how can this man give us his flesh to eat?' And Jesus' reply in 3:5—'Truly, truly I say to you, unless one is born of water and the Spirit...'—runs parallel to his words in verse 53: 'Truly, truly I say to you, unless you eat the flesh of the Son of man and drink his blood...'. In both cases, Jesus sets out the conditions for sharing in the life of the world to come. Now the eucharist too defines the membership of the Christian community.

Once again, then, Jesus addresses two audiences: one in the synagogue at Capernaum, the other in the evangelist's community. If this latter audience is living through a time of hostility and separation from the world, they are at least assured of their solidarity with Jesus and each other in the eucharist. No fellowship could be more real than one in which believers 'eat the flesh of the Son of man and drink his blood'.

6 Going away from Jesus? *Read John 6:60–71*

Again Jesus' message is elusive, but this time it is disciples, not 'Jews', who murmur. The reason, though, is much the same. In verse 42 the Jews saw Jesus as no more than a 'local boy', whose family they knew. In verse 52 they took literally his talk about giving his flesh to eat. Now disciples take offence at the idea of eating his flesh and drinking his blood. What lies behind all this murmuring?

Verse 62 suggests that 'Jews' and now 'disciples' cannot see beyond the earthly to the heavenly. For them there is only one 'story' of Jesus. He is 'the son of Joseph'. He is defined by his family connections. His ministry as a teacher and healer is constrained by the understandable aspirations of Galileans for freedom and food. But there is another dimension to the 'story' of Jesus. As the heavenly Son of man, he cannot be restricted by earthly categories and expectations. Because he comes from God, he must be allowed to redefine human hopes for eternal life. Those who murmur see Jesus solely in terms of 'flesh', in the broader Johannine sense (cf 3:6). 'But the flesh is of no avail; it is the spirit that gives life' (v. 63).

Jesus is not here exalting the spiritual over the material, the ethereal at the expense of the mundane. He is inviting his audience to hold onto both sides of his 'story'. He cannot be defined solely by what he has in common with others—family, region, race; the accidents of birth, life and death. These things are important for Jesus, but as 'spirit' and not merely 'flesh'. They are the stuff of heaven, not earth alone. 'The Word became flesh and dwelt among us, full of grace and truth.' (1:14) The two 'stories' of Jesus should be held together. His audience must learn to let his words and works point beyond themselves to his Father. Then they will understand that God's way of working in, and speaking to, and loving the world is revealed in a surprising way—through the earthly conflict between Jesus and the leaders of his chosen people. As we now see, conflict will issue in crucifixion, yet the fruits of Jesus' sacrifice offer the world the heavenly nourishment it needs if it is to find eternal life.

The disciples who withdraw at this point are at least acknowledging the elusiveness of Jesus' message. It is not easy to grasp. He calls his audience to readjust their vision of God, to realize that much of the time people expect God to do no more than meet their needs and fulfil their aspirations. For the evangelist, ideas like this are sinister and dangerous. They smack too much of the way of Judas. They constrain God by human expectations. The way of Jesus is one of constant revision. Only those like Peter who stay with him can say with the evangelist: 'We beheld his glory'.

This section of the gospel ends with a reminder that it is possible to move away from Jesus. Sometimes people confuse abandoning the church with a drift from Jesus. But these are not necessarily the same. When a church only provides comfort or satisfies convention, it has become an obstacle in the way of Jesus. Some break their ties with the church out of loyalty to God.

The church's responsibility is to enable people to say with Peter: 'Lord, you have the words of eternal life'. What are we to do when a church becomes a hindrance to faith?

Help me, Lord, as I read this gospel
to know the difference between moving
in the mission of your love
and allowing myself to be carried along
by what is no more than comfort or convention.

Further reading

Kenneth Grayston, *The Gospel of John*, Epworth Press 1990, is an accessible and reasonably-priced commentary on the English text.

Mark Stibbe, *John. Readings: A New Biblical Commentary*, JSOT Press 1993, takes a literary approach.

David Rensberger, *Overcoming the World. Politics and Community in the Gospel of John*, SPCK 1988, is a readable collection of essays with a sociological approach.

1 Kings 17—2 Kings 13: Elijah and Elisha

The stories of Elijah ('My God is Yahweh') and Elisha ('God is salvation'), which are sometimes called 'the Elijah Cycle' and 'the Elisha Cycle', cover the period in the Northern Kingdom from about 874 to about 798BC, spanning six reigns and two dynasties. Elijah's chief follower was his successor Elisha, who in turn had disciples. It seems likely that apart from some Court records the narratives about these two great prophets were in the main preserved by their disciples for future generations. Like other stories of remembered heroes, they contain accounts of miracles—five for Elijah, ten for Elisha: stories which, like those surrounding the Exodus, the life and resurrection of Jesus, and the birth of the early church, mark a time when the faith of God's people is being tested. The intention is not to glorify Elijah and Elisha, but rather to demonstrate divine power at a period when visible reminders of it are much needed. How far we take these stories literally depends on our attitude to the supernatural; but we might bear in mind that at this distance it is difficult if not impossible to distinguish between history and legend. If we 'write off' all such accounts in these chapters as pious embroidery we are in danger of forgetting that God has always used miracles to teach us truths about himself, and of losing sight of the serious political and spiritual messages which they contain.

Elijah, the subject of our first week's readings, appears without introduction or family background except that he comes from 'Tishbe in Gilead', which is east of the River Jordan (1 Kings 17:1). Later generations believe that he will return as the forerunner of the 'Day of the Lord' (Malachi 4:5, 6), but during his lifetime he is presented as the opponent of idolatry in Israel, not afraid to challenge even the king on religious and ethical matters. He deals in certainties at a time when, as we shall see, there is much doubt and confusion.

The quotations are from the Revised Standard Version.

1 Drought and provision *Read 1 Kings 17:1–16*

The two protagonists in verse 1 could not be more dissimilar. Ahab, reigning in magnificence in Samaria, has made an alliance with Phoenicia in the north by marrying Jezebel, princess of Tyre. This is politically astute but spiritually disastrous, since Jezebel brings with her the gods of Tyre. Baal, the creator god, demands the same loyalty as Yahweh; Asherah, a goddess sometimes represented by a wooden pole or tree, is Baal's consort. The partnership between the two brings to Israel not only idolatry but the practices associated with attempts to ensure fertility in land, animals and humans. Whilst Ahab promotes this cult (1 Kings 16:32–33) he cannot quite bring himself to abandon Yahweh: 'Ahab served Baal a little' (2 Kings 10:18). So he is both powerful and irresolute—a bad combination. Elijah by contrast is unknown, without any obvious influence, but confident of his status with God 'before whom I stand' (v. 1).

Drought is not unknown in Israel, but a drought of such threatened length and severity would not only be a national disaster but would be seen as divine judgment. Ahab is concerned for his own authority and for his kingdom's prosperity, yet he makes no overt protest when this hitherto obscure prophet delivers his unwelcome message. Elijah seeks to turn the king from idolatry; Ahab can only have wished to render Elijah powerless, hence 'Hide yourself' (v. 3).

'The word of the Lord' is to be a recurrent prompting for Elijah; this time it ensures both his safety and his sustenance. The two stories of divine provision (vv. 6–7 and 8–16) are the first of the miracle stories; they make clear that God has a concern not only for his servant but also for the woman and her son who help the stranger although themselves destitute and belonging to an alien race. Faith and obedience are seen to be rewarded.

2 New life *Read 1 Kings 17:17–24*

Another calamity—this time in the home of Elijah's hostess. Opinions differ on the age of the boy ('child' can also be translated 'young man' or 'youth'), on the exact nature of the tragedy, and on Elijah's part in remedying it. Is the boy actually dead? If not, is the prophet's action 'contactual magic' by which strength is transferred from a healthy to a sick body (a practice documented elsewhere, especially in Babylonian texts)? Is it resuscitation after a period of unconsciousness? Or is the story included to balance the similar miracle later performed by Elisha (2 Kings 4:18-37)? What is clear is that the mother and the prophet both believe the boy to be dead, and that at that time and in that culture death is understood to take place when breath leaves the body.

The mother's reaction (v. 18) is understandable. First, she reflects the current and persisting belief (see John 9:2) that sickness and death are a punishment—perhaps in her case for some hidden sin 'brought to remembrance'. Second, thinking her misfortune must be caused by his presence, she blames the 'man of God'. Her relief when the crisis is over is equally human but even more confused. Elijah is still 'the man of God' (which might apply to any devoted servant of the Lord), but she acknowledges that he speaks God's word.

The story, like the rest of this chapter, demonstrates that Yahweh, not Baal, is the giver of life. He controls the dew and rain, he provides for his servants, he has authority over death. It is part of the continuing process of teaching that he is compassionate—not an automaton mechanically punishing sin. And it underlines Elijah's vocation to breathe new life into God's child Israel, who is becoming lifeless because of the loss of the true faith.

3 Unhelpful attitudes *Read 1 Kings 18:1–2, 17–29*

We return (vv. 1–2) to the main theme of these chapters, the control of the rains. Time has passed, the famine is more severe, and Elijah and Ahab blame each other for the disaster.

Ahab (v. 17) accuses Elijah of 'troubling' the nation (literally 'bringing to ruin'; the word is used elsewhere of those who by their conduct bring down the wrath of God—see Joshua 7:26). Elijah retorts that the real calamity is the idolatry which comes from unfaithfulness to God's covenant. However, at the same time he suggests a way of settling the matter, since the real conflict is not between king and prophet but between Baal and Yahweh—indeed, Ahab disappears from the story at this point until the drama is over. Mount Carmel is chosen as the setting for the contest probably because, lying on the border between Israel and Phoenicia, it is acceptable to both parties. 850 prophets (maintained by Jezebel, as Elijah scrupulously points out) represent Baal and Asherah; Yahweh is championed by 'all Israel', which must mean a representative assembly since there is neither time nor space to gather the whole nation.

Nobody comes out of it very well. Elijah castigates the Israelites for 'limping with two different opinions' (v. 21), and challenges them to declare for one or the other deity, but he receives no response. The prophets of Baal, although given every chance (they choose their own sacrificial animal so that there can be no suspicion of Elijah producing something imperfect) also 'limp' (v. 26)—the same word as in verse 21 but this time describing a strange ritual dance. They then manifest some of the unacceptable phenomena of worship—cutting themselves with knives (v. 28), a practice forbidden in Israelite law (Deuteronomy 14:1), and 'raving on'—a term used for the ecstatic conduct from which Elijah seeks to dissociate his own prophecy.

Yahweh and Baal are judged by the behaviour of their followers, and, as can happen at any time, they are not well served.

4 Yahweh is God *Read 1 Kings 18:30–46*

Among the Canaanite gods, Baal is worshipped as the one who rides on the clouds, sets his thunderbolt in the heavens, and understands the lightning, so proof of the supremacy of Yahweh or Baal depends not only on fire consuming the sacrifice but also on the ending of the lengthy drought.

The events on Mount Carmel raise questions: about the authenticity of the miracle (was the sacrifice set on fire by lightning or even assisted by Elijah pouring spirit rather than water around it?); about the ethics of the mass killing of the prophets of Baal ('instant' retribution for idolatry rather than the prospect of eschatological judgment sits uneasily on the Christian conscience); about Elijah's own style (is he indulging in the ecstatic prophecy of which he allegedly disapproves when he runs to Jezreel—a distance of 17 kilometres—without stopping?). Yet the significance and outcome of these events must be more important than the 'mechanics'. The twelve stones (vv. 31–32) symbolize a future nation united in the worship of Yahweh; the simple and brief prayer (vv. 36–37) contrasts with the raving of the Baal prophets; the 'fire of the Lord' (v. 38) and the acceptance of the sacrifice signal Yahweh's power over nature not only in the wilderness, as demonstrated in previous miracles, but in a settled agricultural community; and Elijah's epic journey is proof of his commitment as the agent of Yahweh and his hopes for a similar commitment on the part of the king and his servants. Above all, it is the ending of the drought, rather than the sending of the fire, which demonstrates the control which Baal may claim, but which Yahweh wields, over the forces of nature.

5 Reaction, re-creation and recommissioning

Read 1 Kings 19:1–18

The length of time covered in this chapter is subject to question (verses 1–3 may describe quite a long period, and the 'forty days' in verse 8 can be a symbolic term for a considerable time), but the sequence of events described is realistic. As often happens, after triumph comes despair. Exhaustion, fear, depression, loss of appetite, self-pity and lack of confidence somehow change Elijah's perception of a decisive victory for Yahweh into a temporary setback for the supporters of Baal.

What has caused this change? The message from Jezebel is succinct and frightening; her irrationality and unpredictability are such that even Elijah quails before her, and the contest between Yahweh and Baal becomes a struggle between Elijah and Jezebel. The words in verse 4, like the words of anyone in despair, deserve to be taken seriously. Elijah's prayer—and that of others before and since—is simply not to wake up in the morning.

His first instinct has been to distance himself from Jezebel; his next need, in common with many who seek release, is rest and food. These are supplied—either supernaturally or by the kindness of human beings ('angels' can also mean 'messengers' or 'servants'), so he can now make the journey to Mount Horeb, which is Mount Sinai where Moses traditionally received the Law.

Here, matters take on their true perspective. 'What are you doing here, Elijah?' (v. 9) is God's invitation to reassess the situation. Protected by a cave from the direct presence of Yahweh, just as Moses was once hidden in 'the cleft of the rock' (Exodus 33:22), Elijah is not slow to respond. But now with hindsight the cause for concern has shifted to Israel's apostasy, to the desecration of the sacred places and the martyrdom of Yahweh's prophets. In spite of Elijah's zeal ('jealous' can be used in a good as well as a bad sense) he sees himself as a threatened minority of one.

The loud cosmic events, again reminiscent of Sinai (Exodus 19:18–19) demonstrate God's power but do not speak with his voice. That comes in a 'sound of fine (or 'thin') quietness'—the total, yet somehow audible, silence which (often after a long struggle) can bring our most intimate experience of God. And the final rehabilitation is not retirement or even recuperation, but a fresh commission. Elijah is given three tasks; he will live to carry out only one of them—the appointment of his successor—though eventually all are achieved. How he feels about this is not recorded, but he receives both a gentle rebuke—there are still many who have not turned to false gods; and God's reassurance—he is well able to ensure the survival of his people (v. 18). With this knowledge, it now seems possible to 'go, return on your way' (v. 15).

6 A question of ethics *Read 1 Kings 21:1–19, 27–29*

The rights and wrongs of this dispute can be variously interpreted. Is Ahab an insensitive tyrant 'pulling rank' in order to appropriate the vineyard (probably the product of generations of work) for a vegetable plot and at the same time to undermine the importance in Israelite society of a family's tenure of its ancestral land? Or is Naboth a disobliging nuisance who refuses a reasonable offer (it is usual for a green, shaded garden to be planted alongside a royal palace)? Whatever the answer, both men are within their legal rights, the one to ask for a sale and the other to refuse it.

Now things go wrong. Ahab, whilst outwardly accepting the decision, reacts badly to being thwarted (v. 4, see also 20:43), clearly lacking any deep respect and value for the laws by which Israel lives. When questioned by Jezebel he tells her less than the whole story (v. 6). Jezebel cares nothing for these God-given principles governing life in the community; her concept of authority derives from her home country Phoenicia, where the king is divine or semi-divine and therefore his word is law. The consequences of this conflict of ideologies are dire. Jezebel (with at least Ahab's tacit consent) organizes events which lead to Naboth's public disgrace and death.

Many questions are left unanswered. What is the offence which leads people to believe that a solemn fast is justified? Why is Naboth disposed of with such suspicious ease on the word of two witnesses who are known to be 'base (literally "worthless") fellows'? (v. 13). Why has the supremacy of Yahweh demonstrated on Mount Carmel not been applied to the everyday practice of the Law of God? Popular opinion does not easily change, especially when it is reinforced by fear and subservience, and the connection between religion and morality is not easily made, even in Israel.

A regime which uses the Law as a tool of royal power and endangers the moral basis of society will face the consequences in the fairly distant future, but they are still inevitable. Such a dynasty cannot continue; yet the mercy of God is present even in this sorry story. Ahab is genuinely responsive to Elijah's words, and a 'stay of execution' is granted. For Jezebel, who presumably refuses to listen, there is no escape (2 Kings 9:30–34). Part of our freedom is to refuse to acknowledge our sin and accept God's forgiveness.

GUIDELINES

The strength and influence of Elijah remind us that God uses ordinary people, neither well known nor in powerful positions, to challenge evil and to bring about change. This chosen servant is not free from fear and weakness, yet he obeys God's commands and defies personal danger and abuse. For 'God chose what is low and despised in the world... to bring to nothing things that are, so that no human being might boast in the presence of God' (1 Corinthians 1:28, 29).

13–19 JULY 2 KINGS 2:1—13:21

1 An end and a beginning *Read 2 Kings 2:1–14*

This passage has been called 'an attempt to describe the indescribable', yet human experience recognizes and agrees with much of what happens.

Elijah knows that his work is done; so does Elisha; so do the 'sons of the prophets' (one of the bands of prophets who figure during the dynasty of Ahab's family). The author knows it too; the 'whirlwind', or stormwind sometimes associated with the coming of God (see Isaiah 29:6; Ezekiel 13:11), is not delayed until the moment of maximum dramatic impact, but is mentioned in verse 1. There is no attempt to overplay the fitting and inevitable end of a chapter in Israel's life.

Elijah takes Elisha on a taxing journey, following some of Israel's first steps in the Promised Land in reverse (Joshua 5–8), and reenacting that earlier crossing of Jordan. Here there is a further link with Moses; just as Moses used his staff, the symbol of his office, to part the Red Sea waters (Exodus 14:21, 22), so Elijah uses his no-longer-needed cloak to part the river. At each stage he gives Elisha the chance to stay behind (perhaps echoed in Jesus' threefold request to Peter in John 21:15–17).

If these are tests, Elisha passes them all, but as the moment of parting approaches, given the opportunity, he asks to inherit a 'double portion' of his master's spirit. This is not presumption, but an eldest son's request to receive the appropriate share of his inheritance according to the Law (Deuteronomy 21:17). Yet Elijah cannot grant this, for unlike a conventional bequest, his spirit is not his to pass on. Only God can give the gift of the Spirit, and he promises to do so if we ask him (Matthew 7:7–8). The 'chariot of fire and horses of fire' do not take Elijah to heaven; they separate him from Elisha and cut him off from human sight.

And now the test is whether Elisha can 'see' (literally 'comprehend') (v. 10) the spiritual world. He shows his understanding first by his profession of faith, 'My father... the chariots of Israel and its horsemen', and then by tearing his mantle in demonstration of his own unworthiness. Having 'seen' and understood, he takes up his office by courageously using Elijah's discarded cloak to make a way for himself through the river, into a life which will be different, but full of promise and challenge. God sometimes challenges us to new responsibilities and service by means of traumatic events.

2 Elisha takes over *Read 2 Kings 2:15–25*

Elisha's authority is established in different ways in three stories.

First, the 'sons of the prophets' must accept that Elijah has gone. Intellectually they understand this, but Elijah has been known to disappear and reappear before (see 1 Kings 18:12). Whether they cannot cope emotionally, or whether they are anxious not to dishonour his corpse by leaving it unburied, they demand a search. Elisha knows the exercise is pointless; knows, too, that the 'Spirit of Yahweh' to which they refer (v. 16) is not an external, physical, but a spiritual, indwelling force. But eventually (v. 17), pressed until he is 'ashamed' (probably 'until he has not the heart to refuse', as in the Revised English Bible), he wisely agrees to the search. Grief takes many forms; denial is one, and must be worked through.

The first miracle (vv. 19–22) was probably selected to show that Elisha's powers were used, as Elijah's had been, to help others, not himself. The local water is 'bad' and said to be causing sterility and even miscarriages among animals and humans. Research suggests that some springs can have this effect because of contact with radioactive geological material, and that sudden cleansing can be due to a geological shift. Whatever the later explanation, people will remember that Joshua cursed Jericho (Joshua 6:26) and that the curse needs to be removed. Elisha takes a new, uncontaminated bowl, and salt (which was used for its hygienic and preservative qualities and also used in a ritual of separation: a city 'sown with salt' is separated from common use and from its past—see Judges 9:45). So Jericho is separated from Joshua's curse and made habitable again. But the prophet makes it clear (v. 21) that it is *God's* action which blots out the past and gives a fresh start.

It would be convenient to avoid the story in verses 23–25 of mischievous children cruelly destroyed because they tease a grown-up about his baldness (often a sign of disgrace in ancient times). The story has been dismissed as 'indefensible from a moral point of view'. However, the word translated 'small boys' can also mean 'servants', or 'young men'. Whether the incident is real or apocryphal it underlines the seriousness of mocking (literally 'insulting') a prophet, which is the equivalent of insulting God himself (see Deuteronomy 18:19). Such derision is forbidden, and must reap the consequences (see 2 Chronicles 36:16; Galatians 6:7).

3 A home and a family *Read 2 Kings 4:8–17*

The stories in the first and last parts of this chapter are reminiscent of Elijah: the provision for a family in need, and the resuscitation of a child. Just as the authenticity of Elijah's activities in 1 Kings 17 has been questioned as introduced to balance Elisha's powers, so Elisha's miracles here prompt the complementary question 'Are they included to raise Elisha's profile and give him status like that of Elijah?' Whatever the answer, Elisha is shown to be at ease in all sectors of society, supporting those who fear Yahweh, and gifted with prophetic and healing powers.

Shunem is on the route between Mount Carmel and Abel-Meholah where Elisha lives. The 'room with walls' (v. 10) built for the prophet on the flat roof-top is permanent, unlike the arbours sometimes erected to accommodate guests. The family is well-to-do, but 'a wealthy woman' (v. 8) can also be translated 'a great lady'; a description justified by her dignified response to Elisha's offer of some return for her hospitality (v. 13).

She has a husband, wealth, status, a supportive family and a faith in God (she refers to Elisha as 'a *holy* man of God', a unique recognition of his special quality). But she has no son to carry on the parents' name and title to their land, and to be a sign of God's favour. Need is not confined to the poor and downtrodden, and Elisha knows that God has a care for all. The reaction to the prospect of a child is reminiscent of Sarah (Genesis 18:12) and Zechariah (Luke 1:18). It is sometimes easier to give, as the family at Shunem have done, without any thought of reward, than to take God's equally freely offered gifts. It is encouraging to know that initial disbelief is not penalized, and does not disqualify us from these blessings.

4 The Israelite prophet and the foreign dignitary

Read 2 Kings 5:1–16

In contrast to the previous chapter, this passage points out that while God cares for the wealthy as well as for the needy, they are not exempt from trouble and sickness, nor are they given special privileges.

The story is full of the unexpected. The high-ranking, successful and favoured soldier is struck down by a serious skin disease (though leprosy as we understand it today was at that time unknown in the Near East). The captive maid advises the Commander-in-Chief. The king of Israel sees the king of Syria's request, accompanied by over-lavish gifts, the silver alone five times the price that Ahab's father Omri paid for the site of

Samaria (1 Kings 16:24), as direct provocation, whilst Elisha, with no armies at his disposal, stays calm and even detached. Naaman expects the prophet to treat him with deference and ask him to do 'some great thing' (v. 13); instead he is told to perform a simple action not unlike the Law's required sevenfold cleansing for leprosy (Leviticus 14:7–9).

Perhaps most surprising are the story's advanced ideas about the universal power of God. This may be because it was written down some hundred years after the events it describes—in the time of Amos, whose thinking was comparable:

Did I not bring up Israel out of the land of Egypt,
and the Philistines from Caphtor,
and the Syrians from Kir?
(Amos 9:7)

It begins by attributing the victories of Syria, the traditional enemy of Israel, to Yahweh's intervention; it continues with the cure of the foreigner, and ends with Naaman's declaration of faith in the God of Israel as the only God, tempered though that may be by some evidence of monotheistic belief in the Syria of his day. Finally, Elisha's refusal to take a present (literally a 'blessing') as a reward for his services contrasts favourably with the attitude of false prophets (see Matthew 7:15) and of his own servant later in the chapter.

Truly, God shows no partiality, but in every nation any one who fears him and does what is right is acceptable to him. (Acts 10:34–35)

5 Contrasting concerns *Read 2 Kings 5:17–27*

Naaman's concern—in common with believers throughout the ages—is to work out how he can worship the God of Israel in a pagan environment. In spite of his affirmation that Yahweh is the only God 'in all the earth' (v. 15) he still wants Israelite soil on which to offer sacrifice. The feeling that the god of a nation is most powerful and immanent on home territory is deep-rooted, and traces of it appear some three hundred years later during the Jews' exile in Babylon (see Psalm 137:4). Naaman also asks for a dispensation to 'bow himself in the house of Rimmon' (probably another name for Hadad, the Syrian god of thunder and rain) when he has to attend his royal master; 'leaning on my arm' (v. 18) may mean not physical support but 'as his right-hand man' (see 2 Kings 7:2).

All is resolved satisfactorily. Elisha's 'Go in peace' is more than a formal farewell; it indicates that the hearer is in covenant relationship with the speaker and with his God, just as 'Is it peace?' (see 2 Kings 9:17–19) is used when opening negotiations.

Gehazi's concerns are as reprehensible as Naaman's are honourable. Possibly resentful that 'this Naaman the Syrian' has received benefits free of charge, he yields to avarice and to deceit. The avarice is the more heinous because he swears his intentions in the name of Yahweh (v. 20); his dishonesty deceives Naaman but not Elisha, who either suspects or receives supernatural warning of his servant's intentions.

We cannot know how or whether Naaman's hopes are fulfilled; we can only note that his thoughts are towards God. We *are* told what happened to Gehazi and his family. It is pointless to try to understand the lengths to which the belief in corporate responsibility is accepted and acted upon in the Old Testament, but we are sharply reminded that sin has consequences, and that these are not always confined to the sinner.

6 Mission accomplished *Read 2 Kings 13:14–21*

Assuming that we accept the biblical chronology, Elisha is now very old, at the end of a ministry of some sixty years. However, his influence in royal circles is still strong; the king addresses him with the same words spoken by Elisha when Elijah departed (2 Kings 2:12). It is an acknowledgment both of the part played by the prophet's inspiration of Israel in her battles against Syria related in previous chapters, and of his value to King Joash, which outweighs that of conventional forces.

Two incidents follow which are sometimes called 'sympathetic magic', but which actually identify with prophetic symbolism—actions which not only illustrate what is to happen, but which are links in the chain of events which bring the outcome. Other, military, examples are Aaron and Hur holding up Moses' hands in the battle with Amalek (Exodus 17:8ff), and Joshua stretching out a spear over Ai before the decisive encounter (Joshua 8:18).

With the windows opened eastwards—the direction from which the Syrians usually attack—and his hand over the king's, signifying identity of purpose, Elisha sees in the shooting of the arrow the sign of complete victory over Syria. But God's will can be thwarted by human timidity and irresolution; when Joash is told to strike the ground with the arrows he uses only three, not the whole quiverful, and the final subduing of Israel's enemy will be brought about not by the present king but by Jeroboam, his ungodly son (2 Kings 14:25, 28). Even a ministry such as Elisha's can end with disappointment; the legacy of victory which he has hoped to leave is defeated by the royal lack of purpose.

Verses 20 and 21 may be part of the hagiography preserved by the prophetic guilds, or they may have been inserted to show that just as Elijah is not reported as dead, so Elisha remains potent in the grave. The verses are reminiscent of the belief, still held today, that the bones of the dead at least for a time retain supernatural power. But whatever their source, they are a reminder that the power of a ministry is not cancelled out by one failure, and that it does not end with the death of the one who exercises it.

GUIDELINES

Far from living under the shadow of his illustrious predecessor, Elisha develops an equally varied and effective ministry, extending it into new fields such as military strategy and the ministry to Naaman, the high-ranking 'stranger' who belongs to Israel's enemy. No task seems too hard for Elisha to attempt, given

God's command and enabling. We can be influenced and inspired or overawed by the example of others perhaps greater than ourselves, but there is a distinctive work for every servant of God who is willing, prayerful and obedient.

1 Peter, Jude and 2 Peter

How can the church survive in a hostile world? As we shall see over the next three weeks, the letters of Peter and Jude offer timeless guidance for Christians struggling to keep their faith alive under attack.

The threat of persecution is the main subject of 1 Peter, while Jude and 2 Peter are more concerned with the dangers of false teaching.

In a nutshell, the letters adopt the same approach to both problems: 'This is the true grace of God. Stand fast in it' (1 Peter 5:12). The readers are encouraged to see how God has kept faith with them; but they are also challenged to show the same faithfulness in return.

These notes are based on the New Revised Standard Version of the Bible.

20–26 JULY **1 PETER 1:1—3:7**

---

1 Peter Introduction

Sent from Rome, after the church there had been persecuted by the Emperor Nero in the mid-60s, the letter warns the Christians in Asia Minor that further suffering is on the way.

Scattered around the provinces of northern and central Turkey, these fledgling churches had little sense of identity. John Reumann comments, 'Culturally, religiously, and socially, these Gentile converts had broken with their old environment... provoking the charge, "You don't party with us any more!"' The letter sees this as their first test. To cope with that—and with any further persecution—they will need to stay close to Christ. Salvation is therefore described as a journey in his footsteps. Like him, they will walk the way of the cross; but they will also be brought home to glory. In the meantime, their life together can be a foretaste of the joys that await them in heaven.

According to tradition, Peter himself was martyred in Rome in that first wave of persecution, which makes his personal authorship unlikely. Yet the letter was sent in his name by those who had known him and listened to his teaching. Their primary aim was to pass on the words of Christ, 'Take up your cross and follow me.' (Mark 8:34)

1 A living hope *Read 1 Peter 1:1–12*

To encourage the faint-hearted, the letter begins with a rousing reminder that God is in charge. It is God who has begun this work in them (v. 2) and despite all their frailties, it is God who will see the work through to completion (v. 5).

This God has touched their lives in three ways in particular. Verse 2 speaks of a church which felt chosen by the Father, made holy by the Spirit, and 'sprinkled with the blood' of Christ (a reference to the story in Exodus 24 where Moses sprinkles the Israelites with blood as a sign of the covenant that God has made with them).

The New Testament contains surprisingly few passages which bring the Father, the Son and the Holy Spirit together, as verse 2 does here. It is an important reminder that the doctrine of the Trinity was not handed down from on high. Instead, it grew out of the experience of the church, as the earliest Christians described the different ways in which they had encountered God in their midst.

In all these ways, the readers are reminded of their true identity. As Christians, they have been reborn into the new covenant that God has made with his people. From this perspective, neither death (v. 3) nor the various trials of life (v. 6) are to be feared. Through all these fleeting experiences, God is bringing them home. That is what is meant by the word 'salvation', and it is not only a future hope (v. 5)—it is also there to be glimpsed in the present (v. 9).

Verses 10–12 explain how this salvation was prophesied in the Old Testament. In the wilderness, and later in the time of the exile, the Israelites dreamed of coming home to the land that God had promised them. But the prophets pointed beyond that, to a Messiah who would bring the whole world home to God (see Isaiah 49:6), and this is the good news which is now being announced (v. 12).

2 Born again *Read 1 Peter 1:13–25*

How does this new Christian identity express itself? Today's passage offers three guiding principles, which bear a marked resemblance to Jesus' summary of the law in Mark 12:29–31.

The first (vv. 13–16) urges them to live as holy people. The quotation 'You shall be holy, for I am holy' may be read either as a commandment (as in its original sense in Leviticus 11:44), or as a promise. This was, after all, written to a community well aware of the sanctifying work of the Spirit (1:2). Yet verses 13–14 suggest that holiness demands a mutual effort, on God's part and theirs: the grace of God is there to help, but they still need a sense of discipline and a determination to leave their old ways behind.

The second principle (vv. 17–21) is that they should remain rooted and grounded in God. Although they are on their way home, they are not there yet (hence the use of the word 'exile' in v. 17). The way of Christ is a hard path to follow. They may be tempted to return to their old ways, or to look for security in material possessions (v. 18). But the letter reminds them that they have been 'ransomed' by the blood of Christ (vv. 19–20). The image comes from the story of the Passover in Exodus 12. Like the Israelites there, they have been set free to begin a new life with God, who alone is their true security (v. 21).

Finally, they are urged to 'love one another deeply' (vv. 22–25). Like the Israelites setting out for the Promised Land, they are on the journey together. One of the privileges of being born again (v. 23) is that they become part of a new family, with a common responsibility to support one another. Again, this is something that God shares. In all their frailty (v. 24) they are sustained both by the enduring word of God (v. 23) and by the love of their fellow human beings (v. 22).

3 Grow into salvation *Read 1 Peter 2:1–10*

'Whoever does not receive the kingdom of God as a little child will never enter it.' (Mark 10:15) While the Christian journey may begin with simple child-like faith, this passage and others (e.g. Hebrews 5:12–14) point to the need to grow up with God. Although this is an important question for individuals, the emphasis here is on the Christian community: were the churches in Asia Minor growing in their life and worship together? Or was their common development held back by the divisive behaviour mentioned in verse 1? As we read the passage, we may like to ask these questions about our own churches.

Verses 4–8 offer an architect's blueprint for unity and growth in the church. Christ is the cornerstone (v. 6), the reference point which brings the other stones into alignment with one another. But his work depends on people's willingness to fit in together. Only then can the house of God take shape (v. 5).

Switching metaphors, the verse then describes the whole church together as a 'priesthood', in which every member, inspired by the same Spirit, shares the task of worshipping and serving God. There is no higher calling, as verses 9–10 make clear. Together, Christians are the people of God, a glorious new society, in which everyone is of equal worth. No one is more important than the rest—all are there simply because of the mercy that they have received.

Above all, they have been chosen together to 'proclaim the mighty acts of him who has called you' (v. 9). The battle lines have been drawn. Those who believe are different from those who do not (vv. 7–8). How will the unbelievers see the light of God's glory, if the people of God fail to show it to them? As we shall see over the next three days, the call to be witnesses in word and deed affects every area of life.

4 Conduct yourselves honourably *Read 1 Peter 2:11–17*

Again, the readers are reminded that they are exiles, far away from their true home (v. 11), but here the full implications of this are spelt out. It makes them 'aliens' in their own society, people of another culture, whose views and values differ widely from their neighbours'.

As we saw earlier, the recipients of the letter were Gentile converts, who had been called to leave their old ways behind. Clearly, their new lifestyle was often criticized by those who did not understand it (v. 12), but they are advised to silence their critics simply by living a good and honourable life. The advice closely resembles Jesus' teaching in Matthew 5:16.

Throughout the chapter, they are urged to remain true to the example of Christ. This is made more explicit in tomorrow's passage, but the same understanding governs all the advice that is given here. Just as Jesus refused to allow the temptations of the wilderness to distract him from his ministry (Luke 4:1–13), so should they (v. 11). And just as Jesus' behaviour impressed those around him, whatever their faith (e.g. the Roman officer in Luke 7, or the Samaritan woman in John 4) so too should theirs (v. 12).

Following on from this, they should also accept the authority of secular institutions (v. 13). The point is carefully argued. Unlike Romans 13, where Paul says that such authorities are appointed by God, this passage leaves the question open. Christians are to keep the law to silence their accusers (v. 15) and to avoid evil (v. 16)—yet the command to fear God clearly takes precedence over the command to honour the emperor (v. 17). Without being directly subversive, the passage raises the possibility that Christians may one day have to choose between the two.

5 Accept the authority of your masters

Read 1 Peter 2:18–25

It's one thing to accept secular authority when it is exercised with a sense of justice (v. 14), but how should Christians respond when such authority is exercised unjustly?

On the surface, the discussion here is about the particular duties of slaves or servants, but verse 16 has just pointed out that every Christian is a servant of God. Again, without seeming too subversive, the letter offers a coded warning to the churches that conflict may be on the way.

The advice is stark. Here too, Jesus' example is to be followed: however unjustly they are treated, Christians are called to bear their suffering without retaliation (v. 21). The description of Christ's suffering (vv. 22–25) uses the imagery of Isaiah 53 to remind the believers how their lives have been changed by Christ's death. They have been freed from their sins and healed (v. 24); and they have been brought back to the 'shepherd and guardian of their souls' (v. 25).

The advice seems to be based on an understanding that human injustice is a worldly and temporary phenomenon, while the justice of God is an eternal reality. This is why Jesus 'entrusted himself to the one who judges justly' (v. 23). As we saw in 1:5, the letter was sent by a community which confidently expected that the 'last times' would fully reveal God's salvation and therefore vindicate those who had followed Christ faithfully. So the readers are urged to trust God in the same way—both for the future, and for the present. The shepherd is with his flock as they make their way home.

6 Purity, reverence and consideration *Read 1 Peter 3:1–7*

Continuing the theme of authority, the letter switches to the subject of marriage. The instructions to wives (v. 1) have a radical edge. In those days, a wife would automatically be expected to adopt her husband's religion. Yet the letter suggests that Christian women may 'win over' their unbelieving husbands by their pure and reverent behaviour (v. 2).

The advice in verses 3–4 may seem overstated to modern ears. Yet the main point is simply that God values the 'inner self' far more highly than outward appearance. Like yesterday's passage, it offers an important lesson for the whole Christian community. What might it say in our own society, where image and style are often valued far more highly than personal integrity?

The reference to Sarah and the 'holy women' in verses 5–6 (presumably the wives of the other leading patriarchs) is curious, given the way in which they often complicated the lives of their husbands! Sarah, in particular, only calls Abraham 'Lord' when she is laughing at the preposterous idea that they might have a child in their old age (Genesis 18:12—the Greek translation familiar to the early church used the word 'Lord' instead of 'husband'). Nonetheless, God's will was fulfilled through them, and the women of Asia Minor are urged to follow their example.

The advice to husbands (v. 7) also extends to the whole community: show consideration and respect to everyone, for they too are 'heirs of the gracious gift of life' in their own right. By implication, the verse may also suggest that Christians have a particular duty to respect those who are less powerful than themselves.

Passages like today's and yesterday's, which contain specific instructions for a society very different from our own, are notoriously difficult. If we take them too literally, we may reinforce discriminatory behaviour which is no longer acceptable. But if we dismiss them entirely, we may overlook the valuable lessons they offer to everyone. Tomorrow's *Guidelines* discusses this more fully.

GUIDELINES

As we have seen, 1 Peter puts forward the view that Christians are 'aliens' and 'exiles' in the world. But did they withdraw from the world altogether? Some of the equivalent Jewish groups of the time did just that. The Qumran community, for example, founded an isolated settlement in the desert by the Dead Sea. Their monastery was destroyed by the Romans in AD68, two years before the temple in Jerusalem met the same fate. Later Jewish groups, like those who followed the Mishnah Rabbis, stayed where they were, but constructed an elaborate system of ritual purification which made their own home a 'temple', and carefully separated them from their 'unclean' neighbours.

By contrast, the New Testament suggests that the Christians continued to live where they were, raising their families, trading in the marketplace, doing the same jobs they did before they came to faith. As 1 Peter suggests, they chose to remain in the world, to witness by 'doing good' (2:12). This meant recognizing and upholding the laws of the state, and also endorsing the 'household code' which had become the norm throughout the Roman Empire. Based on Aristotle's writings some five hundred years earlier, the code maintained that the order of the home reflected the order of society.

> ***Some are fit to rule (free males, owners, fathers), others to serve (women, children, slaves)... Upset the order of the home, people believed, and the whole society was in trouble. (Meeks)***

The early church seems to have glimpsed the scope of the liberation offered by the gospel of Christ (see Galatians 3:27–29), but clearly they came to restrict their own freedom, in the belief that this would make them more effective witnesses to their neighbours. As we have seen, they were prepared to be treated unjustly themselves, after the example of Christ. But how true were they to the vision of justice which he preached and embodied? That leaves an important question for us, some 1900 years later. When should we submit to injustice, and when should we seek to challenge it?

> ***God, grant me the courage to change the things***
> ***I can change;***
> ***the serenity to accept the things I cannot change;***
> ***and the wisdom to know the difference.***

27 JULY–2 AUGUST 1 PETER 3:8—5:14

1 Do what is good *Read 1 Peter 3:8–22*

'Finally, all of you...' The specific advice to slaves and wives is now applied explicitly to every Christian. Within the group, their unity (v. 8) will depend on the qualities of sympathy, love, tenderness and humility that they show to each other. And these same qualities should govern their behaviour to those beyond the group as well. Rather than paying back any abuse they may receive, they should concentrate instead on paying back the blessing they have been promised by God (v. 9).

How is this done? The quotation from Psalm 34:12–16 stresses that 'doing good' matters more than anything else. This will keep them in a right relationship with God (v. 12), and be vital in their witness to others (vv. 13, 15). However they are treated, they are to respond calmly (v. 14) and gently (v. 16).

Humility, tenderness, gentleness, respect: they make a striking set of hallmarks for the people of God. Is our own witness characterized by such qualities, or do we tend to adopt a more confrontational style?

When the letter returns to the example of Christ (vv. 17–18), it chooses to focus on his trial and death rather than his earlier ministry, which *was* often outspoken and confrontational. For the Christians in Asia Minor, however, this was the right message at the right time. Suffering was on the way, and they needed to understand its purpose in order to be fully prepared.

As verses 19–22 explain, Jesus' sufferings occurred in the context of his journey to heaven where he now reigns with God. Because of his suffering, the gate of glory is now open—not only for those who presently believe, but also for those who disobeyed long ago. Like the ark in which Noah and his family survived the flood (vv. 20–21), Christ has brought them safely through the waters of death. Together with all the baptized, they have risen with Christ and can now stand before God without sin.

2 Live by the will of God *Read 1 Peter 4:1–6*

The consequences of yesterday's passage are now spelt out for the readers. They have been raised with Christ, in order to live a new life. It is vital, therefore, that they now leave their old desires behind and do God's will (vv. 1–2).

The same advice was given earlier (1:14) to encourage them to grow closer to God. This time, however, it is also part of their witness to the local community. If they can avoid such 'excesses of dissipation', they will not only surprise their unbelieving neighbours (vv. 3–4), they will also testify to the 'spirit' that lies above and beyond the world of the 'flesh' (v. 6).

As in 3:18, the distinction between the spirit and the flesh is not about the superiority of the spiritual over the physical in general. It refers specifically to the life with God which awaits us once our earthly lives are over. For those who follow Christ faithfully, the salvation of God will be fully revealed. For those who reject Christ, it will be a time of judgment (v. 5). The choice is there for everyone: even the dead have heard the gospel (v. 6; see also 3:19) and been given the opportunity to choose life.

This eternal perspective is offered to help the readers understand the purpose of the sacrifices they are called to make as they follow Christ. Direct suffering is mentioned briefly in verse 1, but further discussion is postponed until later in the chapter. The emphasis here is on a sacrificial lifestyle. In every culture, in every generation, it has never been easy for Christians to avoid the types of behaviour listed in verse 3, especially if they shared those experiences with a particular group of people in the past. Although the passage is clear that such behaviour is now 'off-limits', there is nothing to suggest that Christians should withdraw from such groups altogether. How else can they witness? Hard though it is, we are called to engage with the world.

3 The end of all things is near *Read 1 Peter 4:7–11*

For the first time, the letter mentions overtly the idea which governs so much of its thinking: the end of the age is coming *soon* (v. 7). It is vital, therefore, that the believers should use this time to prepare themselves. In practice this means living 'in the spirit' now—anticipating the unity and worship of heaven here on earth.

Their unity depends on their love for one another (v. 8). Although the passage sets out the ideal, it is wonderfully realistic along the way. They are ordinary, fallible human beings, who will inevitably misunderstand and hurt each other at times. But love—especially when it is expressed in forgiveness and tolerance—can 'cover' such sins, and hold the community together.

Borrowing the imagery of 2:4–10, love is the cement which will hold the stones together when they are in danger of falling apart.

Such love can also be expressed by showing hospitality (v. 9) and serving one another (v. 10). Obviously, Christians are called to be generous with their possessions and gifts—but it is important to receive the generosity of others as well. Every member has a particular gift from God, for the whole body (v. 11).

Sometimes it is harder to be served than it is to serve. We may be frightened to rely on others, in case they let us down. We may be jealous of the gifts they have—gifts which we may lack. We may simply be too proud to admit that we need help. But verse 10 reminds us that this mutual giving and receiving is part of the 'manifold grace of God'. As ever, God's love for us is revealed in practical, tangible ways.

The ultimate aim for the church is that God may be glorified 'in all things' (v. 11). True worship involves action as well as words. If the church in Asia Minor can understand that now, they will be ready for the eternal glory ahead.

4 Sharing Christ's sufferings *Read 1 Peter 4:12–19*

The letter returns to the theme of suffering, this time linking it with the glory that has just been discussed. By sharing in Christ's sufferings, the believers also share in his glory—not only in the future (v. 13) but also in the present (v. 14). It is an important point. Like the people mentioned in the Sermon on the Mount (Matthew 5:1–12), those who are reviled for Christ are 'blessed' on earth as well as in heaven. They will know the presence of God with them.

We saw yesterday how the church's worship was made up of actions and words. Here, suffering completes the picture—this too glorifies God (vv. 15–16). Clearly the passage is not talking about suffering in general. It is talking about the specific suffering that comes from taking a stand for Christ, whose name all Christians bear.

The time of judgment is beginning (vv. 17–18). For the believers, tested by the 'fiery ordeal' mentioned in verse 12 (see also 1:6–7), it will be a time when their faith is found to be genuine. Above all, they will discover how important it is to trust the God who has made them, and remains faithful to them (v. 19).

But what will happen to the unbelievers? The question is raised in verses 17–18, but not answered. This is surprising, given the sense of the quotation from Proverbs 11:31, which clearly suggests that the ungodly will be repaid for their sins, just as the righteous are repaid for doing good. But the letter goes out of its way to avoid condemning the ungodly. All it says is that they will come to judgment (4:5). Might this offer a glimmer of hope to those who do not follow Christ? Will they too receive one last chance, like the dead mentioned in 4:6? Again, the question is not answered here—but it seems fair to say that the possibility is not ruled out entirely.

5 Clothe yourselves with humility *Read 1 Peter 5:1–7*

In case any of the basics get lost as the last times draw near, the elders of the churches are reminded of their calling (vv. 1–2): they are to 'tend the flock of God' willingly and eagerly. Verse 2 acknowledges two of the most common problems for Christian leaders. There is a danger that their hearts may grow cold with time, until all that is left is a sense of duty. And they may end up using their position to satisfy their own desires.

Whether or not they realize it, the elders have great power, and such power needs to be handled very carefully indeed (v. 3). They are not there to dominate the flock. They are there to care for them, and to be a helpful example. This was the model established by Christ himself, the 'chief shepherd' (v. 4), who is leading them home to glory.

Fundamentally, the whole church is called to live with humility (vv. 5–6). This makes sense: if the elders love the people in their care, and treat them with respect, then those who are younger will have no need to rebel against their authority. As the quotation from Proverbs 3:34 reminds them, they should also humble themselves before God—the God who will raise them up on the last day.

Above all, they are reminded that God cares for them (v. 7). The point is made to refresh the elders in their leadership, and reassure the people in their care. Whatever anxieties they have, God is more than able to deal with them.

As a footnote, it is worth noticing the importance of verses 1–2 in the discussions about the letter's authorship. Apart from 1:1, this is the only reference to the apostle Peter in the letter. The writer speaks as a 'witness' of Christ's sufferings (though the word can also mean 'martyr'), and his advice ('tend the flock') is strongly reminiscent of Jesus' charge to Peter in John 21:15–19. The evidence is not conclusive (see introduction), but it seems clear that the readers were expected to have heard about Peter's life, and possibly his death too.

6 Stand fast *Read 1 Peter 5:8–14*

Picking up the advice given in 4:7, the letter reminds its readers of the need to be disciplined and alert. They are not only up against human opponents (v. 8): the devil is looking for every opportunity to devour them. For the first time in the letter, a policy of direct resistance is recommended (v. 9). The vital thing is to remain steadfast in the faith, the very thing which the devil is looking to destroy.

The larger picture is slowly revealed. The Christians in Asia Minor are part of the worldwide church, whose sufferings have already begun. Beyond such suffering, however, lies the prospect of eternal glory (vv. 10–11) and the promise that God will 'restore, support, strengthen and establish' them.

This is why faith is so important. The word means more than belief: it is the active process of trusting God. Believers are called to place their lives in God's hands, and to stick to that decision, come what may.

The letter ends as it began, with a reminder of God's 'grace' (v. 12). The God who has given so much already, and promised even more, can be trusted. They can 'stand fast', in the knowledge that God has already shown his faithfulness to the believers elsewhere (v. 13), who are united with them in the love and peace of Christ (v. 14).

After the epic scale of verses 8–11, it is interesting that the grace and love and peace are expressed in wonderfully ordinary ways—in greetings and kisses, in the loyalty of Silvanus, and in the letter whch he brings. In a hostile world, what better way is there for Christians to encourage and support each other? This is how the love of God is made known to us all.

GUIDELINES

As this week has shown (and next week's readings will emphasize), theories about the 'last times' dominate the writings of the New Testament. Nearly two thousand years later, as we try to make sense of them, it is important to recognize that different writers say different things on the subject.

In 1 Peter, there is nothing to suggest that Christ will reappear on earth. His true glory will be revealed to the believers one day (1:7, 13), but this is part of the inheritance that is kept for them *in heaven* (1:4). The key event here is the resurrection. Since Christ has been raised from the dead (1:3), they know that they too are on their way to something which is 'imperishable, undefiled and unfading'.

Although 'the end of all things is near' (4:7), 1 Peter does not speculate on how the world will end. This is very different from the book of Revelation, and also from Jude and 2 Peter, as we shall see next week. The Christians in Asia Minor were simply told that they would be vindicated at the coming judgment (4:5, 17) and would live for ever in the glory of God (5:10).

This was all they *needed* to know, at the time. So far, they had only experienced misunderstanding and criticism (2:12) but if more intense persecution was on the way (4:12), then they needed that heavenly perspective. They needed to know that death was not the end—but rather the gateway to a life which was far richer and more glorious than anything they had yet encountered.

Although we live in a very different world, this may well be a message that we too need to hear. Our society says very little about death. It has little or no concept of the 'last times', even though we now know that the resources of our frail planet will not last for ever. Above all, the pace of modern life makes it increasingly difficult to find time to reflect on our relationship with the God 'in whom we live and move and have our being'. If we can get the past and the future into perspective, then we may well find—as the early church did—that our understanding of the present age is also transformed.

Almighty God, who alone can bring order
to our unruly wills and sinful passions:
give us grace to love what you command
and desire what you promise,
that in all the changes and chances of this fleeting world
our hearts may surely there be fixed
where lasting joys are to be found;
through Jesus Christ our Lord. Amen

Collect for Easter 4

3–9 AUGUST — JUDE AND 2 PETER

Jude Introduction

The striking similarity between 2 Peter and Jude raises an important question for those who read the two together. Which of the letters was written first? Does Jude summarize 2 Peter? Or does 2 Peter take the original teachings of Jude and rewrite them at greater length, adding one or two extra points along the way?

In recent years, scholars have come to favour the second option. As we shall see, Jude is a letter written in a hurry. It offers an urgent and specific warning about a group of false teachers. As 2 Corinthians 11:4 and 1 John 4:1 also suggest, the ministry of itinerant charismatic teachers often caused great problems for the early church. Jude encourages his readers to ignore their dangerously subjective teachings, and focus instead on the God who has been revealed as Father, Son and Holy Spirit.

1 Trees without fruit *Read Jude:1–13*

Like James, Jude is the brother of Jesus himself (Matthew 13:55), but neither of their letters claims any additional authority from this fact. Both describe themselves as 'servants' of Jesus, and offer greetings to their fellow-believers in a spirit of equality. Jude reminds his readers that God is already powerfully at work in them. Not only are they 'called' and 'beloved'; they are also being 'kept safe' (v. 1). As such, the mercy, peace and love for which he prays (v. 2) are already theirs to be enjoyed.

The letter comes straight to the point. It is vital that they should hold on to this understanding of their faith, because false teachers have stolen in among them (vv. 3–4).

'You will know them by their fruits.' (Matthew 7:16) These people can be identified as false teachers because they use the gospel as an excuse for 'licentiousness', and deny the lordship of Christ (v. 4).

What are the tell-tale signs? Jude highlights their sexual immorality (v. 7) and dismisses them as 'dreamers' (v. 8), which perhaps suggests that they were manipulating the believers with visions, claiming divine authority for their own words. Clearly their irreverence and selfishness also ruined those times when the believers met to break bread together (v. 12).

Throughout the passage, Jude uses various stories from the scriptures to show these people in their true light, and to indicate what will happen to them. Some of his examples are taken from the Old Testament (see Numbers 14, Genesis 6 and Genesis 19), while others come from Jewish apocalyptic writings which were obviously familiar to his readers. Common to them all is the theme of eternal punishment (vv. 6, 7, 11, 13).

Finally, four metaphors from the world of nature spell out the implications for the community (vv. 12–13). These false teachers will not bring refreshment or life to the believers, only damage and chaos.

2 Build yourselves up in your most holy faith

Read Jude:14–25

The first book of Enoch (quoted in vv. 14–15) is another example of Jewish apocalyptic. As we know from the books of Daniel and Revelation, that style of writing often coincided with periods of political oppression. It longed for justice, for the day when the ungodly oppressors would be condemned and the righteous rewarded. Here, the political element is missing, but the note of judgment is retained for those false teachers who have demonstrated their ungodliness again and again (v. 16).

The believers are urged to keep this eternal perspective in mind (vv. 17–18). If anything, the very presence of the false teachers is a sign that the last times are at hand.

For the time being, unity—the true sign of the Spirit—is more important than anything else (v. 19). And their unity will grow if they concentrate on three basic principles: 'pray in the Holy Spirit', 'keep yourselves in the love of God' and 'look forward to the mercy of our Lord Jesus Christ' (vv. 20–21). It is a stunning reminder that the believers are locked into a relationship with the Father, the Son and the Holy Spirit—the God who is protecting them on every side.

Their unity will also grow if they show mercy (vv. 22–23)—not only to those who are wavering, but even to the ones who are leading them astray. As the final hymn of praise suggests (vv. 24–25), God is more than capable of bringing everyone home to glory in the end.

'Be merciful, just as your Father is merciful.' (Luke 6:36) Mercy is more than a theory. In what specific ways has God been merciful to us over the course of our lives? Like Jude, let us offer our thanks and praise for that, and consider how we might show the same mercy to the people around us.

2 Peter Introduction

Although 2 Peter makes use of the letter of Jude, it addresses a very different situation. The false teachers here are not 'off-the-wall' charismatics. Immersed in the secular culture of the day, these people were rational and even sceptical about their faith. How could the apostles' teaching be authoritative, when the 'last times' had failed to appear in their lifetime? And if they were wrong about that, why should the church take any notice of their moral teaching, particularly when it made them look so ridiculous in the eyes of their unbelieving neighbours?

All this suggests that the letter was written towards the end of the first century, which means that Peter himself was probably not the author. (Further questions about scriptural authority and authorship will be picked up in this week's *Guidelines*.) Nonetheless, the letter is sent in Peter's name, probably by the church in Rome, to uphold the authority of the apostles' teaching, and remind the readers that the 'last times' are indeed on their way.

3 Participants in the divine nature *Read 2 Peter 1:1–11*

The letter begins by reminding the readers that their faith is exactly the same as that of the first apostles (v. 1). It rests on the saving work of Christ, who has led them to know God (v. 2) and experience his grace and peace.

From start to finish, his divine power has given them all they will ever need (v. 3). 'Godliness' here seems to mean more than mere holiness, or goodness. Rather, it defines the process by which Christians leave the corrupt world behind and so come to participate in the divine nature (v. 4).

This is very different from other New Testament writings about the Christian life. The Holy Spirit is not mentioned. Instead, the letter borrows the ideas of the Greek philosopher Plato, who argued that the physical world prevented people from knowing their original godlike nature. Like Plato, the letter urges its readers to set their minds on spiritual qualities rather than material things (vv. 5–7)—but these ideas are set in a Christian context. The point here is that these qualities will lead them to grow in their knowledge of *Christ* (v. 8). This will remind them of the forgiveness they have found in him (v. 9), and draw them closer to one another as they follow their original calling through to the end (vv. 10–11).

As Christians, how do we respond to the secular thinking of our day? Rather like Paul during his visit to Athens (Acts 17:16–34), today's passage opens a dialogue with contemporary philosophy. Its ideas are examined with respect, and then set alongside the claims of the Christian gospel, so that each can illuminate the other. In a letter which is all too aware of the dangers of false teaching, it is a courageous approach.

4 Established in the truth *Read 2 Peter 1:12–21*

Against the charge that the Christians were following 'cleverly devised myths' (v. 16), today's passage reminds its readers that their faith is grounded in reality.

Peter himself could testify to that (vv. 12–15). Even if the letter was written after his death, as seems likely, the message was being passed on by the church which had known him, and had heard many times the stories of his life with Jesus.

Those first apostles were 'eye-witnesses of his majesty' (v. 16–18). The story of Jesus' transfiguration (see Matthew 17:1–8) is told with an eye on the future as well as the past: this same Jesus, whose glory and majesty they witnessed on the mountain, will come again in glory to judge the world.

The passage stresses that it was God who appointed Jesus to this task. As such, the second coming, and the judgment which accompanies it, is not a story created by the apostles to frighten people into obedience. It is an act of God, which is on the way.

The Jewish scriptures also testify to this (vv. 19–21—see, for example, Daniel 7:13–14). Countering any suggestion that the prophecies of the Old Testament may have been human rather than divine, the letter stresses that the Holy Spirit was at work both in the initial prophecies, *and* in their subsequent interpretation. We shall see in this week's *Guidelines* how this is crucial to the letter's views about scriptural authority. As verse 19 points out, the light must dawn in the reader's heart as well.

5 The day of judgment *Read 2 Peter 2*

Verses 1–3 identify the destructive elements of the false teachers' message. They deny the saving work of Christ (v. 1), lead people into 'licentious' ways which discredit the gospel (v. 2), and deceive their followers in order to line their own pockets (v. 3).

The main deception concerns the delay in the second coming. In reply to the charge that God has fallen asleep, verses 4–10 offer a stark reminder of the judgment revealed in the Jewish scriptures. Like Jude, the letter uses these stories as cautionary tales. The earthly judgment shown here is a foretaste of the final judgment: the ungodly will be condemned and punished, while those who remain righteous will be rescued (v. 9).

Highlighting the stupidity of these false teachers (vv. 10–16) the letter adds the example of Balaam to the list (see Numbers 22). Even his donkey recognized that he was disobeying God. If the readers are in any doubt about their new teachers, a careful examination of their motives (v. 14) should reveal the truth.

Using the final part of Jude's argument, verses 17–19 confirm the inadequacy of the false teachers' views. While they promise freedom (v. 19), those who follow them will be enslaved by their own desires.

The chapter ends with a stern warning to the believers about the dangers of abandoning the faith. Having known the way of righteousness (v. 21), their disobedience will be viewed far more seriously on the day of judgment. The references to the dog and pig (both unclean in Jewish law) also emphasize the folly of such behaviour.

As we saw in Jude, the false teachers are evaluated in four areas: their doctrine, their conduct, their motives and their results. The list sets a high standard for any teacher or leader. How can we help and support those who teach us?

6 The patience of our Lord *Read 2 Peter 3*

The letter takes up Jude's point, that the false teachers are in fact a sign that the last times are at hand (vv. 1–3). Their claim that 'all things continue as they were from the beginning of creation' (v. 4) ignores the fact that the 'word of God' has spoken (v. 5). He has destroyed his creation once before in the flood (v. 6), and will do so again (v. 7).

If this has begun to make God sound rather monstrous, verses 8–9 quickly introduce a note of compassion. God is waiting patiently, 'not wanting any to perish, but all to come to repentance'. Nonetheless (v. 10), the day will come.

These three verses offer a fascinating glimpse of the way in which the early church began to think about the 'last times' as the years passed by. The letter was written at a time of great uncertainty, after the first generation of apostles had died, which made the prophecy of Mark 9:1 very difficult to understand. While the church continued to believe that the day would come soon, they were beginning to acknowledge that God in his mercy might have other plans.

For the time being, the main point is that the readers should not be led astray by the false teachers' dubious morality. Both now and in the future (vv. 11–14) righteousness is what matters—behaving rightly (v. 11) and being right with God (v. 14). The letter pays tribute to Paul's teachings in this respect (vv. 15–16). Clearly some of his writings were being misinterpreted, but the church in Rome was happy to endorse his letters as orthodox Christian teaching.

In summary (vv. 17–18) the letter looks forward. Rather than losing their way, the believers are urged to stick to the path, and carry on growing 'in the grace and knowledge of our Lord'. How exactly might we do this?

GUIDELINES

As we have seen, this week's readings raise a number of questions about the authority and authorship of the Bible.

2 Peter in particular offers a fascinating glimpse of the process by which the early church weighed up the various teachings on offer. Some were accepted as authoritative, while others were dismissed as being harmful and heretical.

Ironically, 2 Peter was one of the last writings to receive official recognition from the church, because of its similarity to Jude and its doubtful authorship. Yet it was deemed to be valuable precisely because it defined the criteria by which the various writings of the New Testament were admitted into the canon of scripture.

The letter suggests that the teachings of the apostles, including Paul, should be accepted on the same basis as the Jewish scriptures—as being inspired by God (1:21; 3:2, 15). The teaching of the apostles might also include letters which were written in the name of an apostle after his death. We know now that the practice of writing under another person's name was common at the time, as a way of passing on the wisdom of great leaders.

But 2 Peter makes the additional point that the authority of scripture needs to be confirmed by the community which receives it (1:19–21). In other words, the Holy Spirit has to be active on both sides of the process—in the reading as much as the writing. This is as true today as it ever was. As we continue to read the scriptures, let us pray that our understanding may continue to grow and develop under the guidance of that same Spirit.

O Lord, who hast given us thy word
for a light to shine upon our path:
grant us so to meditate upon that word
and to follow its teaching,
that we may find in it
the light that shineth
more and more unto the perfect day;
through Jesus Christ our Lord. Amen

St Jerome

Further reading

Richard J. Bauckham, *Jude, 2 Peter. Word Biblical Commentary Vol 50*, Word 1983.

Wayne Meeks, *The Moral World of the First Christians*, SPCK 1987.

J. Ramsey Michaels, *1 Peter. Word Biblical Commentary Vol 49*, Word 1988.

John Reumann, *Variety and Unity in New Testament Thought*, OUP 1991.

Job

> ***You have heard of the steadfastness of Job and you have seen the purpose of the Lord, how the Lord is compassionate and merciful. (James 5:11)***

Many of us, when reminded of the biblical book of Job, will recall this passage from the epistle of James which speaks of the steadfastness or patience of Job. This phrase has worked its way into our language as a description of one who is extremely, almost excessively, patient in the face of calamity. We need to ask: does Job deserve this reputation or, when we look at the book more closely, does a different picture emerge? Has the tradition represented him fairly or has it in fact glossed over a more protesting strain found in the book?

The book of Job is divided between a prose prologue and a poetic dialogue. The prose prologue contains the main action. The dialogue is less digestible, being fairly repetitive and made up of a number of rather disparate sections. We have a hymn to wisdom towards the end of the dialogue. We have dislocation of some of the speeches in the third cycle which gives the impression of people saying the wrong things. We have the speeches of a fourth friend, Elihu, who appears unannounced and then repeats material. Finally, we have the speeches of Yahweh followed by Job's repentance. As we work through the text we will look at these sections and see how they all fit together.

We also find a number of different themes apparent in the book. The prologue seems to be mainly an airing of the issue of disinterested piety—will Job still trust God even if his family, possessions and health are taken away? At the end of the prologue Job seems to pass the test devised by God and Satan, and the story might have ended there. However, the best is to come, in that the second part of the book, the dialogue, airs issues of innocent suffering and the doctrine of retribution. The question is raised: do good things always come to those who are pious or are the good sometimes wrongly punished? Conversely, are the wicked rightly punished or do they in fact prosper at the expense of the good? And finally at the end of the dialogue the issue changes to that of the relationship between God and Job, representing humanity in general. Is God's justice on another plane to ours? Will we never have any answers to innocent suffering? Or is there an answer to be found in communion with him and humble submission to his will?

The book ends as it began, with a story—this time the restoration of Job to his former glory with a new set of children and twice as many possessions. We might ask whether this is in fact a satisfactory ending to the book or whether there is just a hint of irony in the ending in the light of all that has gone before.

The version of the Bible we will use is the Revised Standard Version.

10–16 AUGUST JOB 1:1—3:26

1 Piety leads to prosperity *Read Job 1:1–5*

The first details we are told are Job's location in Uz, his name and that he was 'blameless and upright, one who feared God and turned away from evil' (1:1). This is the essence of what the narrator is trying to get across here. He wishes to present Job as a model pious man, one with a strong moral character who has committed no sin in the sight of God or humanity. Fear of God is at the centre of Job's concern and from that his ethical behaviour springs. We do not know where the land of Uz is—it might be the area known as Edom, south of Israel. It is interesting that this land is outside Israel. Perhaps it is meant to represent a far-off land, as in legends. The whole prologue has a slightly stylized, folk-tale feel to it. The numbers of Job's possessions are round ones—7,000 sheep and 3,000 camels, for example. The tale is set in the time of the patriarchs, when wealth was measured by numbers of animals. It has a ring of authenticity without claiming to be a strictly historical account. The message here is that piety equals prosperity. It is a natural outcome for a man of good character that he be blessed both in family and possessions. Neither he, nor others, would have expected otherwise. And it is this that is to be undermined in what follows, despite the fact that Job has done nothing wrong.

We are then introduced to the customs of Job's children who used to 'hold a feast in the house of each on his day' (v. 4). It is not clear whether this refers to daily feasting or to feasting on birthdays. The latter is more probable. Clearly the family were close-knit and brothers and sisters enjoyed each other's company. Whilst there does not seem to be a suggestion of excessive feasting here, just in case, Job, as a concerned parent, sanctifies his children after the feast days and offers sacrifices on their behalf. He does pious deeds on behalf of his children. His religious commitment is remarkable. Maybe there is a hint of overzealousness on his part. The purpose of the narrator is clearly to show Job as extra-scrupulous so that in no way can he be seen to deserve the misfortunes to come.

2 Piety put to the test *Read Job 1:6–12*

The scene now shifts from earth to heaven. We move from a scene of domestic bliss to a heavenly council at which the sons of God, probably angels or lesser deities, wait upon God. We are introduced to the 'adversary' or 'Satan', who was probably once one of these sons of God but who has become detached from them and has become God's opponent. We are told of God's pride in Job as there is 'none like him on the earth'. This phrase is usually used of God alone, not of humans, so Job is especially honoured by God. Satan, however, sows the seed of doubt. He questions Job's motive for fearing God, arguing that he merely does it because of the protection God offers. Job enjoys blessing in his work and in his wealth—of course he will be faithful in such circumstances. Satan accuses God of putting a protective hedge around Job which, once removed, will shatter Job's faith in one blow. Issued with such a challenge, God licenses Satan to carry out the test with the proviso that Job's own body is not harmed.

We might wonder what kind of God submits his faithful servants to such a test. Job is clearly an innocent victim, used by God to prove a point in a contest with Satan. There are overtones here of the testing of Abraham in Genesis 22, where a trusting servant is driven to the limits of his obedience to God by being asked to sacrifice his son. And yet in both instances, it is in fact an expression of God's trust in his servant that leads him to allow each of them to go through such a test. And so perhaps we can see the testing in a more positive light. The heavenly prologue functions for the reader or listener in providing us with the reason for the suffering about to befall Job. But of course, Job knows nothing of this heavenly discussion and so when suffering strikes there seems no reason for it, as is the case in our own experience when we suffer.

3 Acceptance in the face of misfortune *Read Job 1:13–22*

The scene shifts back in verse 13 to the earthly domestic scene that we left in verse 5. Suddenly, on to this scene calamity falls. I choose the word 'falls' because this is to echo the Hebrew word used for three out of the four calamities. First, Job loses oxen and asses and the servants tending them when human enemies, the Sabeans, fall upon them and kill them. One messenger escapes to tell Job of their plight. Second, Job loses sheep and more servants when the 'fire of God', presumably lightning, falls from heaven. Third, camels and the servants attending them are lost, this time in a second enemy attack from the Chaldeans. And finally, and most disastrously, the house in which Job's children are feasting falls on top of them as a result of 'a great wind', again a force of nature, probably a tornado. It is interesting that two of the calamities are as a result of human agency and two are seen as from God in being natural disasters. This is perhaps to show the different forms in which disaster can strike unexpectedly at any time, true today just as it was in biblical times.

Job's reaction is to mourn in a public and pious way. He practises the usual traditions of mourning—rending his robe and shaving his head. Tearing the garments is representative of the sudden pain that comes with calamity and shaving the head may be an act of identification with the dead. Job also falls to the ground, probably to denote his submission in the face of God. He then utters what sounds like a liturgical formula, 'Naked I came from my mother's womb, and naked shall I return; the Lord gave, and the Lord has taken away; blessed be the name of the Lord.' (v. 21) He is referring to death when he speaks of returning to the womb. He accepts that God gives blessings and can remove them and he is even able to bless God. It is emphasized in the next verse that Job did not sin or blame God. It is emphasized because piety is the chief factor that the narrator wants to stress here. Job the patient is alive and well—his piety has survived the first test.

4 Illness as the ultimate test *Read Job 2:1–13*

In chapter 2 we find round two of the heavenly scene. There is much repetition here, which has the effect of heightening the drama. We find God again using Job as the model believer and here claiming that Job has passed the test. This is the opportunity for Satan to try a new line of attack: possessions and even offspring are one thing—they are external—but to be attacked physically so that one's body is ill to the point of virtual death is another. 'Skin for skin,' says Satan, in a phrase that may mean that Job will give up all to preserve his own body. God again accepts the challenge, with the proviso this time that at least Job's life is spared. Back to earth and we find Job afflicted with a leprous disease. The exact disease is not stated, but with running sores it cannot have been pleasant! He scrapes the pus out of his sores and sits among the ashes. This may be part of his mourning ritual or it may signify his debasement. Alternatively, it may refer to the heap of dung or ashes usually found at the city gate, on which lepers and other outcasts from the city were found. Job is the victim of a cruel fate.

A new character is introduced in verse 9, Job's wife. It is curious that she has not featured earlier when Job's family was mentioned and that her reaction to losing her children is omitted. It is odd that she too was not removed as part of Job's loss of family—maybe the irony is that it adds to Job's suffering to have her around and to hear her reaction. One is reminded perhaps of the warnings about nagging wives in the book of Proverbs! She advises Job to 'curse God and die'. She is reacting in a hostile way, blaming God. Job chides her and calls her one of the 'foolish women', the antitheses of wise women. Again Job reiterates his acceptance—good and bad should alike be received from God. There is again the emphasis on Job's sinlessness in word and deed.

Finally, we are introduced to the three friends of Job who come from afar to offer comfort. They also adopt mourning rites, identifying with Job's state. It is not clear why they sprinkle dust on their head—it is possibly another way of identifying with the dead. The friends sit on the ground with Job, a sign of humiliation, and are silent with him for seven days and nights. At this stage they appear as sympathetic figures, consoling and quiet and yet present in his need. This is set to change, as we shall see.

5 A lament from the depths of despair *Read Job 3:1–10*

A sudden change comes over Job. We now find him lamenting using a series of dark and disturbing images that come from the depths of a person's despair. No longer is he accepting all that comes to him. Here he utters what sounds remarkably like the curse his wife told him to utter. He curses the day of his birth and the night of his conception in a wish that he had never existed, such is his torment. He desires to wipe the day of his birth from the calendar so that all memory of him is lost. This contrasts vividly with his children's celebration of their birthdays. The day and the night are personified and cursed. He calls upon evil powers that can evoke the chaos monster, overcome at creation by God. He longs for darkness rather than light in a reversal of creation itself.

In fact, although this section has many characteristics of the curse, it is not strictly speaking a curse because it curses the past and not the present or future. Also, it is not a direct curse to God, rather it is a curse on the day of birth. Curses were usually uttered in order to influence or change a situation and were thought to contain power in themselves. We might compare this passage to Jeremiah's curse on the day that he was born (Jeremiah 20:14–18) and with lament psalms, which have a similar pattern. In these verses, then, a very different Job appears—he is no longer patient, he is profoundly distraught. Here we are in the dialogue and we will see how a very different picture of Job is painted. The pious, folk-tale character has disappeared and in his place we have a more real, agonized character who is reacting to suffering in a way that we might perceive as more realistic, at least in the questioning context we find ourselves in today.

6 Death as a release from pain *Read Job 3:11–26*

We now encounter Job wishing he had died at birth. He longs for the peacefulness and quietness of death in contrast to his own torment. He speaks of death as making everything seem futile in comparison—in verses 14–15, all that is left of the great palaces of kings are ruins. Building achievements which incited wonder have all but disappeared. Human acquisitions and effort are in vain. He also wishes that he had been an untimely birth (probably a reference to miscarriage or abortion) because then he would not have been fully formed enough to have survived. He reflects on death as the great equalizer—the prisoner is now at peace with no taskmaster to torment him and the slave is no longer bound to his master. This is a self-lament and wish for death that predominates over other emotions.

From verse 20, Job still longs for death since he no longer knows the path he is following. His old certainties have disappeared and God's hedge around him is now seen as oppressive, contrasting with the protective hedge of the prologue. Such is his pain that he does nothing but sigh and groan. His worst fears have been realized. All he wants is rest, which is refused to him by the pain which he endures, both physically and mentally. Here he is lamenting his lot in the face of God's treatment of him. However, this is not a direct address to God; rather, it takes the form of a monologue. His experience is at the forefront of his concern here, but he uses the opportunity to muse on the fate of humanity as a whole and on the nature and desirability of death. He is not a happy man!

GUIDELINES

We have in the first three chapters of Job been introduced to various different reactions to suffering. Job in the prologue reacts with acceptance and does not waver in his faith. He is prepared to accept God's will for him. For some people this may be how they respond to misfortune, not necessarily understanding it but accepting what God has to give. We also have Job's wife, whose reaction is hostile towards God, again a valid response. We have the initial reaction of the friends, which is to offer sympathy and say as little as possible. We then surprisingly encounter Job in the dialogue, showing a similar hostility to that of his wife. He curses the past that brought him into being and then goes on to lament his fate, longing for death. These are all valid reactions to suffering. Possibly the one that shows a certain protest is a more realistic first reaction than an accepting stance. The latter may occur as a result of mature reflection but is hardly the way most of us feel initially. We have also seen that hardships come from different quarters—some from human agency and some from divine causes. Actions in heaven are hidden from human beings, but the interest and involvement of the divine is centred on humanity. We are not outside God's concern; the question is what our motives are for being faithful to him and how we would react if calamity struck us, as it did Job.

17–23 AUGUST — JOB 4:12—19:29

1 Visions in the night *Read Job 4:12–21*

Here we encounter the first of Job's 'friends', Eliphaz, speaking to Job, having broken the silence that they had kept for a week. The tone of all three friends is one of persuasion and argument.

In this passage, however, we have the description of a visionary experience from God to Eliphaz. He is using this method of a personal revelation from God to give authority to what he wishes to say. He claims to have had truth revealed to him at dead of night. The experience of the presence of God caused his hair to stand up and his bones to shake. His mind was agitated and he suddenly felt great terror. He experiences a breath or cold wind passing before his face. He then dimly sees a figure before him in the half light which utters words to him. That which is revealed is part of the argument used by all the friends. We can compare 4:17–19 with later words from Eliphaz in 15:14–16 and with Bildad's words in 25:4–6.

The crux of the issue is: can a person be righteous before God? In the first part of his speech Eliphaz has established that God does not punish the innocent person. But now he is saying that in fact no person can be innocent and pure. It is of the nature of human beings to err. To be imperfect is part of being created. Even the angels are not pure. We may perceive someone as just, but God's standards of purity are beyond ours. Being earth-creatures, dwelling in houses of clay, humans are fragile and lowly. They die easily, just like moths. The end of human life is compared to the collapse of a tent as soon as the cord holding it in place is ripped up. Eliphaz adds the point that people even die without wisdom, a dig at Job perhaps for not having perceived what he, Eliphaz, has already understood as a result of his vision. This is a very hierarchical view of the world which tends to denigrate human beings.

We might have problems with this view, that seems to portray humans as inherently sinful and hence unable to do anything good. It seems to be reinforced in Genesis 1–11 too that we are fallen beings, fallen from an ideal which we once aspired to but because of our human nature were destined to lose. Job is unhappy with this picture. He refuses to see himself (and the rest of humanity) as inherently sinful. Job responds to Eliphaz's point in 9:2 when he repeats his question, 'How can a man be just before God?' His answer though is rather different. He argues that God's justice cannot be understood; it is on a different plane. How then can human beings ever hope to know where they stand or how to argue with him? He is here stressing the impossibility of talking about the justice or otherwise of God. We have to hold on to our own integrity because that is all we have got. He knows he has not sinned and to that point he holds on as he comes under fire from the second friend.

2 Does God pervert justice? *Read Job 8:1–10*

We now meet the second friend, Bildad, who insists on the justice of God. He accuses Job of speaking false words and scolds him for them. He picks up on an emphasis on correct speech that we find generally in the wisdom literature—proverbs often express the idea of a word spoken correctly having great power, but bad words leading to bad influences. Here Job is accused of windy words, i.e. both violent and empty. Bildad also asks a question, this time a rhetorical one expecting the answer, No! 'Does God pervert justice?' Of course he does not. What happened to Job cannot be unjust because it came from the Almighty God. He argues that Job's children must have sinned; this is why they have died and Job too must seek God. Bildad thus maintains the traditional doctrine of just rewards—to the good come good things, whilst the wicked are punished. Thus if one is suffering as Job is, he must have done bad things. If he is righteous, he will be restored to greater than he was before. God acts according to these fixed principles in the thought of the friends. Bildad here seems more dogmatic than Eliphaz was.

Bildad does not directly accuse Job of sinning, although it is implicit in his suffering. Rather he tries to urge him to 'seek God'. This phrase also recalls Amos 5:6—'Seek God and live'—an antithesis to the words of Job's wife, 'Curse God and die'. Bildad appeals to the past: learn from the wisdom of old, he says, for our lifespan is short. We need to rely on the accumulated experience of past generations. He has a good point here—the wisdom literature shows us that human experience has remained very much the same for thousands of years. Human nature is still as it is described in Job. Many of us would react in just the way Job has in the dialogue. And yet there is a further lesson. Whilst we may learn from the wisdom of the past, we should also learn from its mistakes. Not everything from the past is good. There is a place for fresh thought and new ideas and whilst much will not turn out to be new after all, it is important to guard against being unable to think outside a traditional framework. This is what the friends suffer from. They have a fixed idea of how God deals with humans. It is an easy way of seeing life. But it is an oversimplification and does not allow them to grow in their understanding of the divine. Perhaps we should look at ourselves and ask whether we are too confined within our own traditional frameworks in the manner of the friends of Job.

3 God's ways are secret *Read Job 11:1–20*

We now encounter Zophar, who also accuses Job of too much talking, of babbling even. He speaks bluntly to Job, telling him that he has no right to read God's mind. It is all very well saying he is innocent but if God could speak he would show Job that he is not. In fact it is blasphemous of Job to be maintaining his innocence when it is clear that he is guilty. Zophar even suggests that Job is suffering less than his guilt deserves. He then launches into a description of the hiddenness of God's purposes, along much the same lines as Eliphaz. God's knowledge lies at the limits of human understanding, higher than heaven, deeper than Sheol, the place of darkness where the dead go. It is wider than the earth, which was at that time regarded as flat, and broader than the sea. God acts in judgment to punish worthless people, often perceiving what human beings cannot perceive.

Zophar makes the comment that 'a stupid man will get understanding when a wild ass's colt is born a man'. The point of this is that a stupid man will therefore never get understanding, since what is proposed is impossible. Could this be a little jibe at Job? He then calls on Job to look towards God, stretching out his hands in supplication. Repentance is what is needed, then he will get the security he needs. There will be no more fear or misery. All will be rectified. It is an attractive picture—security, light, happiness, hope, protection, rest. The reference to light is an interesting recalling of Job's previous desire for darkness in chapter 3. These are the blessings that the wise person can expect. 'But the eyes of the wicked will fail,' he warns. The wicked are trapped and they have no hope left but to die. Severe warnings indeed!

4 The funeral sentences *Read Job 14:1–17*

These verses from Job have become famous for the part they play in the funeral service. They are seen as unrelieved pessimism. Job is at a low point and is reflecting on human life and its brevity. Human life on the scale of things is fleeting and miserable. Like a flower that grows up, blooms and then quickly withers, so is the human being who has a brief prime and then gradually withers away with old age. The person then becomes a shadow, a non-entity, only remembered in the minds of others. They believed at that time that at death a person went to a land of shadows where there was no communication with God, a kind of underworld of neither heaven nor hell, only non-existence. Here Job stresses the fleeting nature of human life in order to ask why God bothers with human beings. Why does God bring a person into judgment? He wonders why God troubles to deal with humans who do not have a chance from the start and are totally in God's control.

There are overtones of Eliphaz's pessimism about the sinful nature of humanity here, and yet Job is even more pessimistic in that he sees God as hedging a person in so that he has no freedom. Instead of God's continual eye on humans being a good thing, as in the psalms, God's attention is unwanted by Job and is seen as oppressive. He begs God to look away so that he may enjoy life for once! Much of this is the opposite of what we are used to hearing about God from biblical figures and is an expression of Job's protest, his despair and his wrestling with God. Job goes on to compare human life with that of a tree which, even when cut down, will shoot again in time. When human beings die, however, that is the end—there are no second chances. Job longs for death for a while, just whilst he is suffering from God's anger, and then for rejuvenation like the tree. But of course he is asking for an impossibility. He has a vision of God calling and Job answering, and of God protecting him as he used to. All transgressions would be forgotten. And so Job wavers from deep despair to a more hopeful note, but it does not last. The chapter ends with more despair.

5 God is on the attack *Read Job 16:6–22*

Just as we thought we were hitting the bottom of the pit of despair, Job goes further. He now launches into a tirade against God. His pessimism is gone; now he is on the attack again, waging a protest against his unfair treatment. He complains that when he speaks he does not feel better, nor does he feel better when he doesn't speak—there is no satisfying him! He accuses God of wearing him out. He has no friends. His body is a wreck. He accuses God of tearing him apart, likening him to a wild beast. He is upset at the way others are treating him, with no respect, in complete contrast to his rank in society before. They see him as a wicked man and so strike him. He feels given over to the wicked. He recalls the time when he was favoured, which is such a contrast to the way things are now.

He accuses God of breaking him in pieces and of being the archer, his arrows pointing at Job's chest. He uses violent images of kidneys being slashed open and gall on the ground, possibly a reference to the effects of his illness. God is a warrior breaching a fortified city and Job the city in whose walls the breaches have been made. He is in mourning, in sackcloth and ashes, he is in grief and despair. Darkness is already settling on Job's eyebrows, perhaps a foretaste of the death to come. What has he done to deserve this? He is after all an innocent man. This picture of God as the tormentor of Job is a radical departure from usual pictures of God. God seems to have turned malevolent and we have here a frightening description of the dark side of God. God is persecuting an innocent man according to no moral code that anyone can work to. How can a human being cope with this and still retain faith in God?

6 My redeemer liveth *Read Job 19:23–29*

At last we seem to have a moment of optimism to relieve the gloom and deep-seated despair that we have encountered in recent chapters. This passage is also famous—made most famous by Handel in *Messiah*, in which it is taken to refer to Christ: 'I know that my Redeemer liveth'. Many do not realize that, in fact, it comes from the book of Job. Job asks to be able to write his words down so that they last for ever, so that, in case he dies, he will one day be vindicated. He has a moment of optimism when he states that his Redeemer or Mediator lives. He means here that justice will prevail somehow and that even if God himself seems to have turned nasty, there will be some justice from one who will mediate between him and God. This translates easily into the message of the New Testament that Christ mediates between God and man and takes on the sins of the world to close the breach between the earthly and the divine realms.

What does it mean here, however? It may be that God and the Redeemer are one and the same, rather than there being a third person brought in. If this is the case, then Job is turning his thoughts more positively to the possibility of eventual vindication by God. This has traditionally been seen as a passage about the afterlife, since it says, 'After my skin has been destroyed… then I shall see God'. However, it could simply be referring to Job's illness. We have seen elsewhere that he is fearful of death—this is the reason he wants his words to be written down, in case he dies before vindication. Another crux is the phrase 'from my flesh' which could be translated 'outside my flesh', again meaning after death, but alternatively means 'from my fleshly body', i.e. whilst I am alive. The vision is of vindication by God. God is on his side and the thought of that makes his heart faint. He closes with another warning to the friends—if they persist in persecuting him, let them beware they do not also become victims of persecution.

GUIDELINES

We have now encountered the characters in the dialogue section of Job. The three friends are seen to represent traditional ideas about reward and retribution. Their line is that Job must have sinned and that is why he is suffering in this way. Job consistently maintains his innocence and wavers from the deepest despair to trust in God. This reflects the stages of our own dialogue with God. A relationship with God, just as with human beings, is not monotone and one-dimensional. Rather it is constantly changing depending on the situation in which we find ourselves and depending on our own understanding of our plight. Through this process of lament, despair and complaint, Job is gradually coming to a deeper understanding of his relationship with God. His speeches get longer and those of the friends get shorter as he leaves their arguments behind. At the end of the dialogue there is considerable mixing of speeches and people seem to be saying contradictory things so we will leave these sections aside next week and go on to the final chapters of the dialogue and the climactic reply of God.

24–30 AUGUST — JOB 28:12—42:17

1 Where shall wisdom be found? *Read Job 28:12–28*

We find in chapter 28 of Job a separate hymn to wisdom, possibly a later addition in the text, but functioning here as a reflection on the nature of the wisdom quest. It seems to support much of what we have already been told by the friends, and by Job, that God's ways are hidden. It supports what we find in the book of Proverbs about God being at the limits of the wisdom quest—at the end of human understanding, there stands God. This poem speaks of the human quest to find wisdom but one which is ultimately frustrated by God. Human beings do not know the way to it. It is not in the sea; it cannot be bought or compared to precious jewels and metals; its price is beyond anything. It is hidden from birds and beasts, even from the places of the dead which are personified here. God alone holds wisdom in his hand. He sees everything. He made everything. He is the Creator. The hymn speaks of the impossibility of the wisdom quest and seems to have a negative tone, and yet the imagery is rich and the poetry beautiful. The quest is negative until the last two verses which suddenly speak of the ability of humans to find wisdom if they trust in God.

This solution was to become increasingly popular as the answer to the problem of hidden wisdom and is found in Proverbs 8, in which the figure of Wisdom mediates between God and humanity. The fear of the Lord is true wisdom which is accompanied by righteous deeds. Keep on the straight and narrow and gradually God's wisdom will be revealed to you. It seems we are back to the doctrine of reward and the words of the friends. This hymn in fact shows the tension between knowledge of God, which goes only so far from the human side, and those vast areas of knowledge that belong only to God. It is that realm that Job seeks to understand in his suffering and it is that realm that the friends think they can pin down by limiting God's justice, although they too have moments of realizing, as Job does, that God's justice is greater than ours and is in a far greater context.

2 A final plea *Read Job 31:29–40*

In chapters 29–31 we encounter Job in a final plea to God. In chapter 29 Job looks back on the time when he was in God's favour. It was a time of protection, of light rather than darkness, of friendship and family harmony. He was respected by all in society. Now he is mocked and hated and he is full of affliction. Chapter 30 describes how he cries to God but remains unanswered. Again he charges God with turning cruel. In chapter 31 he cites various things that he might have done wrong for which he could justifiably be punished. The inference is that he has done none of these things and is innocent. He says in verse 29, 'If I have rejoiced at the ruin of him that hated me...' He has done none of these things. He has not cursed anyone. He has always been generous to strangers and to the needy. He would deserve punishment if he had hidden transgressions but he has always been honest. He has not kept secrets. He again longs to be heard and longs to know the cause of his suffering. He wishes to know, then he could own it and hence justify himself. It is the not knowing that is racking Job with anguish. Finally Job mentions his agricultural activities in which he has done nothing wrong: 'If I have eaten its yield without payment… let thorns grow instead of wheat' (vv. 39–40). But of course he has done none of these things. At this point his words cease and we can imagine Job finally spent of his energy and his words, waiting for something to happen.

3 Another helpful friend? *Read Job 33:1–18*

Suddenly in bursts the youthful Elihu, unannounced, with a few words to say. This section is often regarded as an interpolation because it seems to repeat much of what went before and to anticipate the climax to come in the words of God. He claims not to have come forward to speak before because he felt he should let his elders speak first. But now the time is ripe. He is concerned to stress his sincerity and that the source of his words is God-inspired. He tells Job not to be fearful of him. He reveals that he has heard what Job has had to say. He knows that Job claims to be innocent and that he sees God as his enemy. However, he too argues that God is greater than man. His picture of God is similar to that of Eliphaz: a rather frightening picture is painted of God appearing to people in the night. God appears to deter humans from the evil actions they might want to do. God has a hand therefore in persuading human beings towards righteousness. This is a slightly new angle because it suggests that God actively promotes righteous behaviour rather than just urging it. He suggests that God speaks in more than one way—one conscious, the other unconscious and barely perceptible by human beings. This is to prove God's superiority and his elusiveness in the face of Job's plea for innocence.

4 Where were you at creation? *Read Job 38:1–18*

At last God appears and answers Job. He appears in a whirlwind and is very much the Creator God here, describing his actions on man's behalf purely in natural terms. There is no salvation history here as in many parts of the Old Testament. Job seems to be scolded here: 'Who is this that darkens counsel by words without knowledge?' God could be referring to Elihu here, although Job seems more likely, since the whole debate seems to centre on the two of them. Again the message is that God's knowledge and power is greater than that of human beings. God asks Job questions that he would never be able to answer because they are impossibilities. 'Where were you when I laid the foundation of the earth?' Who is Job to question God who is the Creator and has been here from eternity working out his purpose? There follows a description of creation which has many similarities with both Psalm 104 and Genesis 1 in an ordering of the actions that led to the making of earth and seas, light and dark. He asks, 'Have you commanded the morning since your days began and caused the dawn to know its place…?' Maybe this hearkens back to Job's cursing of the dawn on the day of his birth.

This creative pattern is linked up with the good moral order in which there is no place for the wicked. Thus the principles of retributive justice are upheld in the very created order itself.

Job is challenged to declare if he knows what God knows. Job is thus humbled in a display of God's creative power and omniscience. God goes on to describe the creation of the animals and the overcoming of chaos monsters. Job is thus silenced into submission. He says in 40:4, 'Behold I am of small account, what shall I answer thee?' There is no reply to this approach. Not only are God's purposes greater than ours, but his actions are on an entirely different scale. It puts Job's complaints into perspective. Who is he in the overall order of things? Who is he to question the justice of a God who set up all the orders in the first place?

We might ask whether this is an answer to the problem of undeserved suffering. Partly perhaps, in that we will never know all the answers, but one can't help wondering if this display of power is either helpful or enlightening for Job. Some argue that it is the fact that God appears rather than what he says that is important. At least he does appear, rather than leaving Job hanging in the air with all his questions. And yet in a sense Job is left with all his questions unanswered, because God does not give him the answers he requires. Rather he sidesteps Job's questions in his rehearsal of his actions in creation. The differences between God and humanity are made clear here—we are not to think we can limit God or fit him into the religious script with which we are working.

5 A time for repentance *Read Job 42:1–6*

We now encounter Job's repentance. In 40:1–2 he began to make moves in this direction. Now after a second speech of God he admits that God's power and purposes are undeniable. He quotes God's first words: 'Who is this that hides counsel without knowledge?' (v. 3) He recognizes that he has questioned beyond the limits of his understanding. He realizes now the full wonder of God's actions in the universe. He says an interesting thing, which is that he had 'heard of thee by the hearing of the ear, but now my eye sees thee', which suggests that his understanding of God had been by hearsay alone. His actual witnessing of God's presence is thus a much more profound experience for him. His wish for God to answer him has been granted since he has received his answer and yet it has also been exceeded by the profundity of his experience of God. He now despises himself even more for having questioned in the way that he did and he repents.

In fact, however, we have seen how he grew through his questioning, so it was not altogether a bad thing. Protest has led on to a deeper faith and understanding. But with the hindsight of what he now perceives about God's greatness and his own humility in the face of it, his questions and complaints are made insignificant by comparison. There is a message here for us that it is right to question and challenge God and to attempt to seek understanding through any means possible and yet, at times, there are no answers. Although one may be tempted to give up on God, an alternative is to do as Job does and to repent on one's knees in the face of the greatness and glory of the divine. At least Job has received an answer from God and this acts as an antidote to his pain and serves as the basis for a renewed relationship with God.

6 Rewarded twice over *Read Job 42:7–17*

We now come back to the Job of the prologue and epilogue. The style is once more in prose. Verse 7 is an important verse because it seems to vindicate Job for what he has said over the friends. The friends are scolded by God for not having 'spoken of me what is right' as Job has. This is a surprising statement because all along the friends seemed to be in the right to maintain the traditional dogma. Job seemed to be in the wrong in his complainings and in his view of God as his tormentor. Here there is a complete reversal. At last Job is told that he was right to question and that the friends were wrong. Job is now told to make a sacrifice on behalf of them all and to atone for the friends as well as himself. All the animosity between Job and the friends is gone, but they are brought low and he is lifted up. He is then restored to prosperity in a seeming reinstatement of the system of just rewards. We have just spent the dialogue overturning the system. How is it that it now seems to be alive and well? We must remember that we are back in the prologue and epilogue, where the natural outcome must be the restoration of Job. He has passed the test with flying colours. How else could the book end?

And so we have the required happy ending. Job's brothers and sisters are mentioned for the first time—so he didn't lose all his family after all. His wife is not mentioned. The brothers and sisters shower him with gifts. He ends up, in true folk-tale style, with twice as many animals as he had before and with a new set of children. He has seven sons and three daughters and we are told the names of the daughters, a surprising touch. We are also told that Job gave them an inheritance as well as their brothers, perhaps to demonstrate Job's excessive generosity. We are also told of their beauty. Finally we are told of Job's longevity that allowed him to see many generations of children—the Hebrew idea of blessing and of continuation of a part of oneself after death. He eventually dies happy, 'an old man and full of days'. A very different scenario from the black pictures of death left behind in the dialogue.

GUIDELINES

We have encountered many contrasts in our journey through Job. On the one hand is a right relationship with God and the happiness that can bring. This extends to other people and good relationships with them. It extends to moral behaviour and how we treat others, showing charity to the poor and generosity of spirit to all. This is in contrast to a life racked by pain and fear and darkness, one in which God is absent and in which people become tormentors of each other. We too have a choice about how to lead our lives and how to influence society for good or bad. We also have a choice as to how to respond to suffering. Are we going to be like Job the patient, accepting stoically all that comes our way? Or are we more like Job the protester, waging a battle against God and other people, but gradually coming to a deeper understanding and a calmer acceptance as a result of the trials? Again it is our choice. We may not ever have all the answers—they may be hidden from us, just as ultimate wisdom is in God's hands. But that doesn't mean giving up the quest to understand and the desire to obtain meaning in life. We must live life to the full and never give up hope in the creator and giver of life, even in our darkest moments.

The Bible Reading Fellowship
Peter's Way, Sandy Lane West, Oxford, OX4 5HG
ISBN 0 7459 3272 X

Distributed in Australia by:
Hodder Headline Australia, 10–16 South Street,
Rydalmere, (Locked Bag 386), NSW 2116

Distributed in New Zealand by:
Scripture Union Wholesale, PO Box 760, Wellington

Distributed in South Africa by:
Struik Book Distributors, PO Box 193, Maitland 7405

Publications distributed to more than 60 countries

Acknowledgments

Cover photograph: Jon Arnold

Printed in Denmark

SUBSCRIPTIONS

❑ I would like to give a gift subscription (please complete both name and address sections below)

❑ I would like to take out a subscription myself (complete name and address details only once)

❑ Please send me details of 3-year subscriptions

This completed coupon should be sent with appropriate payment to BRF. Alternatively, please write to us quoting your name, address, the subscription you would like for either yourself or a friend (with their name and address), the start date and credit card number, expiry date and signature if paying by credit card.

Gift subscription name ____________________

Gift subscription address ____________________

____

____________________ Postcode ____________

Please send to the above, beginning with the September 1998 issue:

(please tick box)	UK	SURFACE	AIR MAIL
LIVEWIRES	❑ £12.00	❑ £13.50	❑ £15.00
GUIDELINES	❑ £9.60	❑ £10.80	❑ £13.20
NEW DAYLIGHT	❑ £9.60	❑ £10.80	❑ £13.20
NEW DAYLIGHT LARGE PRINT	❑ £15.00	❑ £18.60	❑ £21.00

Please complete the payment details below and send your coupon, with appropriate payment to: **The Bible Reading Fellowship, Peter's Way, Sandy Lane West, Oxford OX4 5HG**

Your name ____________________

Your address ____________________

____

____________________ Postcode ____________

Total enclosed £ __________ (cheques should be made payable to 'BRF')

Payment by cheque ❑ postal order ❑ Visa ❑ Mastercard ❑ Switch ❑

Card number: ☐☐☐☐ ☐☐☐☐ ☐☐☐☐ ☐☐☐☐

Expiry date of card: ☐☐☐☐ Issue number (Switch): ☐☐☐☐

Signature (essential if paying by credit/Switch card) ____________

NB: BRF notes are also available from your local Christian bookshop.

GL0298

This page is intentionally left blank

BIBLE READING RESOURCES PACK

A pack of resources and ideas to help to promote Bible reading in your church is available from BRF. The pack which will be of use at any time during the year includes sample editions of the notes, magazine articles, leaflets about BRF Bible reading resources and much more. Unless you specify the month in which you would like the pack sent, we will send it immediately on receipt of your order. We greatly appreciate your donations towards the cost of producing the pack (without them we would not be able to make the pack available) and we welcome your comments about the contents of the pack and your ideas for future ones.

This coupon should be sent to:

The Bible Reading Fellowship
Peter's Way
Sandy Lane West
Oxford OX4 5HG

Name ____

Address ____

____

____________________________ Postcode _______________

Please send me _____ Bible Reading Resources Pack(s)

Please send the pack now/ in____________ (month).

I enclose a donation for £_______ towards the cost of the pack.

GL0298 The Bible Reading Fellowship is a Registered Charity

This page is intentionally left blank

BRF PUBLICATIONS ORDER FORM

Please ensure that you complete and send off both sides of this order form.

Please send me the following book(s):

		Quantity	Price	Total
2523	Confirmed for Life *(S. Brown/G. Reid)*	_____	£2.99	_____
3253	The Matthew Passion *(J. Fenton)*	_____	£5.99	_____
3509	The Jesus Prayer *(S. Barrington-Ward)*	_____	£3.50	_____
3286	Ultimate Holiday Club Guide *(A. Charter/J. Hardwick)*	_____	£9.99	_____
3295	Livewires: Footsteps and Fingerprints *(R. Sharples)*	_____	£3.50	_____
3296	Livewires: Families and Feelings *(H. Butler)*	_____	£3.50	_____
3522	Livewires: Friends and Followers *(S. Herbert)*	_____	£3.50	_____
3523	Livewires: Tiptoes and Fingertips *(B. Ogden)*	_____	£3.50	_____
3549	Livewires: Trackers and Trainers *(R. Sharples)*	_____	£3.50	_____
3550	Livewires: Searchlights and Secrets *(J. Hyson)*	_____	£3.50	_____
3565	Sometimes the donkey is right *(B. Ogden)*	_____	£3.25	_____
3566	Best friends *(B. Ogden)*	_____	£3.25	_____
3568	Barnabas and the Stars *(T. Davies)*	_____	£2.99	_____
2821	People's Bible Commentary: Genesis *(H. Wansbrough)*	_____	£5.99	_____
2824	People's Bible Commentary: Mark *(R.T. France)*	_____	£7.99	_____
3258	People's Bible Commentary Luke *(H. Wansbrough)*	_____	£7.99	_____
3280	People's Bible Commentary: 1 Corinthians *(J. Murphy-O'Connor)*	_____	£7.99	_____
3281	People's Bible Commentary: Galatians *(J. Fenton)*	_____	£4.99	_____
3297	People's Bible Commentary: Revelation *(M. Maxwell)*	_____	£7.99	_____
3545	People's Bible Commentary Nahum–Malachi *(G. Emmerson)*	_____	£7.99	_____

Total cost of books £ _________

Postage and packing (see over) £ _________

TOTAL £ _________

See over for payment details. All prices are correct at time of going to press, are subject to the prevailing rate of VAT and may be subject to change without prior warning.

NB: All BRF titles are also available from your local Christian bookshop.

GL0298 The Bible Reading Fellowship is a Registered Charity

PAYMENT DETAILS

Please complete the payment details below and send with appropriate payment and completed order form to:

The Bible Reading Fellowship,
Peter's Way,
Sandy Lane West,
Oxford OX4 5HG

Name ______________________________

Address ______________________________

____

______________________ Postcode ______________

Total enclosed £ __________ (cheques should be made payable to 'BRF')

Payment by cheque ☐ postal order ☐ Visa ☐ Mastercard ☐ Switch ☐

Card number: ☐☐☐☐ ☐☐☐☐ ☐☐☐☐ ☐☐☐☐

Expiry date of card: ☐☐☐☐ Issue number (Switch): ☐☐☐☐

Signature (essential if paying by credit/Switch card) ______________________

POSTAGE AND PACKING CHARGES				
order value	UK	Europe	Surface	Air Mail
£7.00 & under	£1.25	£2.25	£2.25	£3.50
£7.01–£14.99	£3.00	£3.50	£4.50	£6.50
£15.00–£29.99	£4.00	£5.50	£7.50	£11.00
£30.00 & over	free	prices on request		

Alternatively you may wish to order books using the BRF telephone order hotline: 01865 748227

The Bible Reading Fellowship is a Registered Charity